LABOUR
THE PRICE OF POWER

John Horgan

Gill and Macmillan

Published in Ireland by
Gill and Macmillan Ltd
Goldenbridge
Dublin 8
with associated companies in
Auckland, Dallas, Delhi, Hong Kong,
Johannesburg, Lagos, London, Manzini,
Melbourne, Nairobi, New York, Singapore,
Tokyo, Washington
©John Horgan 1986
5   4   3   2   1
0   7171   1442   2
Print origination in Ireland by Design and Art Ltd
Printed in Great Britain by
Richard Clay (The Chaucer Press) Ltd, Bungay, Suffolk

Contents

To Mary

Introduction

SOME time in 1976, an interminable Parliamentary Labour Party meeting was taking place upstairs in that part of Leinster House known as the 1932 Annexe. The normal difficulties of running the PLP were exacerbated, on this occasion, by the fact that this was not the customary room for the meeting. There was no physical focus of authority and both the PLP chairman and the party leader, Brendan Corish, were lost somewhere in the crowd.

Justin Keating, then Minister for Industry and Commerce, unexpectedly leaned over towards me and passed me a note on a torn-off scrap of paper. 'Please', it said, 'resist the temptation to resign.'

The temptation, as it happened, had not occurred to me. Less than a year in the party I was still, perhaps, more an onlooker than a participant. In truth, there was plenty to observe. It was only later, when the extent of the internecine warfare to which all political parties are prone had become clear to me, that I fully understood the vestigial sense of despair, tinged with cynicism, that had inspired the note. For the fact is that the Labour Party, as well as occupying a unique place in the Irish political spectrum, is also, for most of those committed to the idea of radical change in society, the irreplaceable touchstone of political *angst*. For many people on the Left, it has traditionally been the party one would never dream of joining, the party one is thinking of leaving, or the party one has just left. Nonetheless it continues to exist, staggering from one vicissitude to the next, often down but never quite out.

Ten years ago when I joined the Labour Party, one of the people who welcomed me remarked that nobody who joined the party at that juncture in its history could be accused of being an opportunist. Labour was then, by common consent, at a low ebb. It was an integral part of a government which, in the wake of the

1

horrendous price rises after the oil shocks of 1973 and 1974, looked on the verge of becoming the most unpopular government in modern Irish history. There were even times when it appeared as if the general torrent of abuse would sweep the Labour Party away completely. It was being abused by its own Left wing for having allegedly knuckled under to Fine Gael, and by Fine Gael supporters for having insisted on the supposed ideological strait-jacket of a wealth tax. Fianna Fail, with that inconsistency which is the special privilege of all centre parties whenever they happen to be in opposition, was accusing Labour alternately (and occasionally simultaneously) of doctrinaire unreality on the one hand and selling its socialist soul on the other. In the wings, knives were being sharpened for what was—correctly—seen as the inevitable return of Labour to the opposition benches it had occupied for the previous sixteen years. The place for a young man or woman with political ambitions, it was clear, was elsewhere. One zealous supporter of Fine Gael, horrified by what he saw as an illogical decision, said cheerfully that Fine Gael could have promised me a seat for life.

In fact the transition from being an independent member of the Seanad, to which I had been first elected in 1969, to member of the Parliamentary Labour Party, had not been that difficult to make. An independent candidacy had been dictated in 1969 partly by the traditionally non-party (as opposed to non-political) nature of the National University of Ireland constituency, and partly by personal preference. Journalists have almost always declined overt identification with any political party, no matter where their sympathies might actually lie, because of an unwillingness to allow the integrity of their journalism to be called in question. As a working journalist dealing with contentious issues of education and religion, this was a real consideration. The dilemma became sharper in 1973, when the general election coincided with a decision by *The Irish Times* to launch a weekly education newspaper (*The Education Times*), of which I was to be the editor. Negotiations about the appropriate relationship which should subsist between politics and journalism produced, eventually, an editorial contract which expressly forbade the editor of the new paper to join any political party but allowed him to remain as an independent member of the Oireachtas.

Joining the Labour Party in September 1975 effectively broke

2

that term of the contract. In a sense, it was not that journalism had become less important, but that politics had become more so. As someone who had been charting the turmoil affecting the Catholic Church since the middle sixties, I had been struck by the Goya-esque figure of Noel Browne as he strode out, time after time, to do battle with many of Irish society's monoliths. For quite other reasons, the keen political intelligence and salty humour of Frank Cluskey had introduced me to a Dublin working-class Labour tradition of which I had been largely unaware, and which (without romanticising it) remains an effective political force. In six years in Leinster House, in particular, two factors had combined to force a decision. One was the experience in relation to a number of legislative measures—the first attempt to change the law on contraception, a bill to force companies to disclose payments they made to political parties—put forward in the Seanad by a small group of senators including Mary Robinson and myself. From Fianna Fail and Fine Gael these measures elicited either thinly disguised hostility or polite waffle. The Labour Party, even though it was then in government, was the only party to give them even a guarded and very hesitant welcome. In line with its own procedures, such pieces of draft legislation were considered in due course by the PLP. Frequently they were not even reached on the PLP agenda—a turn of events which caused political neophytes from the Seanad no little bafflement. More and more frequently, sitting on the leather-covered armchairs outside the PLP meeting room waiting for the end of yet another meeting, I reflected rue-fully on the fact that the case for whatever piece of draft legisla-tion was at issue was probably being made, on the other side of the door, by someone who was markedly less familiar with it than its sponsor. That door came, in a sense, to symbolise a barrier to any real political influence.

Of even greater significance was the growth of a realisation that many of the issues with which the small group of independent Senators had become associated, and which had been wholeheart-edly taken up by at least some sections of the media, did not amount to anything like a coherent and comprehensive political programme. The issues of the late sixties and early seventies in Ireland were not just the 'liberal' issues—contraception, religious liberty, clerical control of education—even though in an over-whelmingly Catholic country the impact of the Vatican Council

3

could make it appear that this was so. Not even the blather, hot air and shadow-boxing in Leinster House could totally conceal, even from a political novice, that economic issues lie at the core of political activity, although, being complex issues, they do not attract the same kind of media profile as other controversies. Consideration of how power is exercised in society, of how resources are allocated, by whom and to whom, must lead inevitably to an examination of the source and modality of power, and to an assessment of who gains and who loses from the multiplicity of political decisions that are taken in and out of government. The realisation, too, that the structures of society are not graven on tablets of stone, but are products of their time and of the influences that shaped them, provides an introduction to the science of political relativity—to the complex relationships between powerful interest groups and the structures of society within which they operate in defence of their own social and economic interests. The concept that many of these structures not only could but should be changed in the interests of social and economic justice was Damascene in its impact. Suddenly, liberalism by itself was no longer enough. Even as I took the decision, I reflected on an experience which had in some sense pre-figured it: a reporting assignment for *The Irish Times* quite a few years previously, in which I had been sent to cover a prolonged miners' strike at the coalmines in Arigna, County Leitrim. That particular assignment was like travelling through time, and the conflict between coal-owners and coal-miners took on a Dickensian atmosphere that underlined the realities of power and ownership in a particularly dramatic way.

The Labour Party in 1975 was a party marked, for the first time in almost two decades, by the scars of government as well as by those of opposition, to which many of its supporters (but few of its public representatives) had become accustomed. Ten years previously, it had set its face against the idea of participation in government. Two years after that, it had come out of the political closet by boldly labelling itself a socialist party, albeit one whose policies were, in the words of one of its officers, closely modelled on the papal encyclicals. It was a party which had seemed, in the late sixties, to begin to catch a popular mood. There were even some hardy souls who hinted in the press in 1969, at the possibility of an overall Dail majority for what appeared to be a splendidly

4

refurbished political movement. In a sense, the Labour Party of this particular period could be regarded as an international graft onto the fairly moribund Irish body politic. The Vatican Council provided a new context, together with the irreverent table-turning of the students in Paris and elsewhere (not excluding Earlsfort Terrace), and, last but not least, the emergence and growth of an urbanised Irish middle class. Many of the latter were removed totally in place, and at least partially in spirit and ethos, from their rural or small town origins, but they formed a new element in the political equation, even if it was one whose volatility could not be accurately calibrated. It was a period of economic growth, of growth in the numbers in the public service and in the range of services provided. The facts of growth both helped to disguise the continuing inequalities of the ways in which the fruits of the growth were being distributed, and encouraged a hitherto unknown degree of risk-taking. Suddenly, it seemed, anything and everything was possible.

Six years later, huge elements of that precarious structure had crumbled, and the decade from 1975 to 1985 was to be as fraught for Labour as any other decade in its history, with the hopes of the previous decade all but extinguished, and the party itself reduced to a squabbling and incoherent group of people who looked as if they would never again seize even an increment of political power. Its political territory was being invaded and colonised, on the Right by Fine Gael under Garret FitzGerald, and on the Left by Sinn Fein The Workers' Party, as it then was. All in all, it seemed like a tattered remnant of something that might have been, a party that was there for the taking.

This, at any rate, is the picture which is presented with some frequency to the Irish electorate, not only by members of other political parties, with an obvious interest in such a portrayal, but by commentators and others who are never slow to do double duty as grave-diggers whether the occasion demands it or not. The media image of the Labour Party has rarely been as good as it was in the heady days of 1969. More recently, it tends to be treated with condescension, friendly or unfriendly as the case may be. Its remorseless internal quarrels, gnawing away at its capacity to win votes and seats, are seen by *The Irish Times* as beneficial to the quality of political life in the long run. Its willingness to join with Fine Gael in government is greeted with an appropriate nod of the

5

head by Independent House, which will simultaneously (as it did after the November 1982 election) run two editorials, one welcoming the formation of the new government, the other taking Labour to task for insisting on a property tax. But, just as society in Ireland itself has changed over the past two decades, so has the Labour Party, and so has the broad political movement—if that is not too strong a word—of which it claims to be the standard-bearer. Is Labour now doomed to remain the half-a-party in what some political scientists have described as Ireland's two-and-a-half party system—too big to be obliterated, but too small to make the great leap forward of which some of its followers have always dreamed? Or is there another future for this, the oldest party in the state? One thing alone is certain: the emergence of the Progressive Democrats, and Dr FitzGerald's publicly expressed willingness to go into coalition with this new party if the circumstances are appropriate, must at the very least make even the most committed coalitionists in Labour wonder whether it is time to change horses before the animal they are riding dumps them unceremoniously into the nearest hedge.
into the nearest hedge.

This book sets out to chart a future for the Labour Party against the background of an analysis of its immediate past and of contemporary Irish society. It takes as its starting point the conviction that one of the most important things to remember about Irish politics is precisely that they are Irish. While all socialist parties claim to operate within an international as well as a national perspective, there is clearly no simple, universally applicable socialist solution to political or strategic problems created by local sets of circumstances. And, if Irish experience has taught us anything, it is that our circumstances can be quite excruciatingly local.

This book does not set out to be comprehensive, but at the same time it is more than a personal memoir. As an exploration of some of the more intractable questions in Irish politics, it is intended as a contribution to the solution of those problems, rather than an attempt to exploit them.

1

Electoral Failure and the Search for Judas

BAD NEWS travels fast, and in February 1986, when the see-sawing public opinion polls indicated that Labour's national support had sunk to a miserable 4 per cent, the news of an unpublished section of that particular poll swept through the party like a brush fire. It indicated that if an election produced results in line with the poll figures, Labour would return to the Dail with only five deputies—Mervyn Taylor, Dick Spring, Frank McLoughlin, Frank Cluskey and Liam Kavanagh.

Even without being aware of these predictions in detail, the average Labour Party activist, in the years since 1969, has been in the position of someone watching the bathwater swirl away without being able to find the plug. With only two exceptions, the graph of support for the party since 1969 has pointed depressingly downward.

The party's vote had in fact been growing in the four general elections between 1957 and 1969. It went from 9.1 per cent to 17 per cent in that twelve-year period. But the next twelve years saw the process reversed, and by the 1981 general election the figure was back to 9 per cent. There have been four elections since 1981—two general, one European, and one local—and in all four the party's vote has hovered around the 9 per cent figure.

Of course you can prove almost anything from figures. It is not the case, for example, that participation in coalition governments has been universally disastrous for Labour—although you have to go back to 1948 to find a coalition from which Labour emerged stronger than it had entered it. Equally, it could be argued that advocacy of coalition does not, of itself, spell universal disaster. In 1973, as in 1954, the Labour Party actually increased its number of TDs (although in 1973 its share of the vote declined since the previous election) despite the fact that it campaigned explicitly on

7

the desirability of a coalition government. By going back to 1965, and by concentrating on the number of seats won rather than on the party's share of the vote, it could be argued that the 1965–69 policy initiatives and position on coalition had been a serious electoral disadvantage. In 1965, after all, the party had won twenty-two seats—the highest total in modern times—and in 1969 it had declined, dramatically in view of the expectations expressed at that election, to eighteen seats. A supporter of this point of view could argue, in addition, that the party's high vote in 1969 was due less to its policies or to its stance on coalition than to its decision to put up candidates all over the country, including several in no-hope constituencies. Ninety-nine Labour candidates went forward in 1969, more than double the number in the previous election; and the overall high poll for Labour masked a related and simultaneous slump in the average number of votes per candidate nationwide. In the 1965 election the average number of votes per Labour candidate was almost 4,500. In 1969 it slumped to just over 2,600, rising to 3,300 in 1973 and to 3,400 in 1977.

To some extent, of course, these trends are self-explanatory and do not afford scope for conclusive assumptions about the nature and extent of Labour Party support among the electorate. The low vote per candidate in 1969 can be put down to the policy of putting up 'no-hope' candidates simply to fly the flag: in future years, it could be argued, such a policy would have paid dividends and new Labour seats would eventually have been created where none had existed before. Accurate or not, the latter argument was never put to the test. The loss of confidence in the party was so great, it seemed, that never again would it stick its collective neck out in quite such a dramatic fashion. Equally, the rise in the average vote per candidate since that time can—particularly since it has been accompanied by a decline in the number of seats—be attributed to retrenchment rather than to electoral success as such. In fact it is probably true to say that Labour's decline has been in some ways greater than the actual figures would suggest, because, quite apart from the decline in its percentage share of the vote, its decline in terms of seats has occurred over a period when the number of seats in the Dail was actually substantially increased. The fact that Labour failed to gain at all from the additional seats to be fought for (Fine Gael seems, of all the parties, to have gained the most from this development) indicates strongly that had the Dail membership remained at its original total, Labour representation would have decreased even more sharply, and that the increase in the total number of Dail seats actually helped to cushion its decline.

As against that, it is certainly true that the misfire of the celebrated 'Tullymander' seriously affected Labour. James Tully, as Minister for Local Government in 1973–77, masterminded a plan to return the coalition to power on the basis of an extensive revision of the Dail constituencies, increasing the number of three-seaters. The success of this strategy relied on two factors—a continuing and healthy supply of first preference votes for each of the coalition parties, and a strengthening of the transfer pattern between them. The transfer pattern improved, but only between Fine Gael and Labour, helping to create or safeguard Labour seats in Dublin in particular (South-East, Ruairi Quinn; South, myself; and Dun Laoghaire, Barry Desmond). But weakness in the Labour–Fine Gael transfer pattern, combined with the slump in first preferences, meant that many of the three-seaters 'flip-flopped' the wrong way, giving Fianna Fail a far greater majority in seats in 1977 than its vote actually warranted. The euphoria of that government, which lasted effectively until the results of the first pre-election opinion poll reached the Cabinet just after the Dail had been dissolved, prevented the emergence of a realistic perspective on the risks involved. Brendan Halligan, who claimed the Galway West constituency as his own special contribution to Labour's prospects (it stretched way down into parts of Clare where Galwegians had never set foot) was to claim later that he had warned Tully of the dangers involved, but the Cabinet was clearly united on this course of action. Flip-flop or not, however, it did not prevent the survival of John Ryan in North Tipperary, where he performed a political Indian rope trick of amazing dexterity. At the previous (1973) election, he had scraped home by only 143 votes, but when the first count was announced in 1977, it looked as if his goose was well and truly cooked. In order to secure election on the last count, he needed a transfer rate from David Molony's surplus of no less than 82 per cent. The pundits all said that it could not be done. In the event, he secured 87 per cent, and stretched his final winning margin from 143 to 184 votes. The sophistication of the electorate in that particular election can be clearly seen from the fact that of 2,000 votes transferred during

9

the various counts, only *nine* were non-transferable! John Ryan's success notwithstanding, this final demonstration of the politicians' desire to distort the effect of PR probably helped to hasten the day when the revision of the constituencies was to be carried out by an independent Commission. The two successive revisions which have been carried out by this Commission have in fact also tended, if anything, to soften the impact on Labour of the loss of its electoral support nationally.

There has been no shortage of explanations for this decline. The difficulty is that few of them are compatible with each other and that none of them, as yet, commands majority support within the party.

To take them in no particular order of importance, the first explanation is that which was publicly advanced by Brendan Halligan and—to a lesser degree—the party chairman Michael D. Higgins, in the wake of the 1977 election results: the party had not failed the people—the people had failed the party. On an election special programme the night the results came in, Brendan Halligan —who had failed to get elected in Finglas, a constituency he had been nursing assiduously for some years—spoke passionately about his belief that the Irish people should feel ashamed of themselves for what they had done. He appeared, however, less like a latter-day Yeats from the stage of the Abbey Theatre ('You have disgraced yourselves again!') and more like the somewhat bruised political animal he undoubtedly was. More recently, he has returned to the same theme. Speaking to a public meeting of the Labour Party's electoral commission in December 1985, he argued strongly, 'I am no longer prepared to submit to the thesis that Labour has failed because it hasn't, over the years, addressed the issues which need to be addressed. I think society generally hasn't been interested: its attention is elsewhere. Irish society is not interested in policy issues which normally excite the electorate of other countries, straightforward social and economic issues. The Labour Party is an issues-orientated party but Irish society is not interested in issues. Labour does not belong to the apolitical majority.

The thesis that a party's failure to win votes is principally a failure on the part of the electorate (to put it more colourfully, perhaps, the idea that the Irish Labour Party is the cure for which there is no known disease) is, to put it mildly, a novel one. More-

10

over, it is one which is unlikely ever to garner substantial support within the party because of its clear implication that the party will never achieve majority status in the Dail, or anything like it. In their bones, many Labour activists may actually feel this, or may at any rate feel that such a breakthrough will certainly not be achieved in their lifetime, if ever: but to say so publicly would be to remove too much of that basic motivational drive without which any political party will inevitably perish.

Some activists have maintained that the party's successive failures have been due to an absence of policies: but as there seems to have developed an inverse ratio between the number of policies developed and promulgated by the party, and the number of votes it actually receives, this school of thought has been effectively muted, or has merged with the anti-coalition group, which sees the party's participation in various coalition governments since 1973 as the source of all its misfortunes since that date. It is difficult to say, in a shorthand sort of way, which of the party's luminaries has been most closely associated publicly with this position, one of the reasons being that since the party's openness to coalition has been unbroken (although not unchallenged) party policy for fifteen years, many of the more passionate anti-coalitionists have simply decamped. Matt Merrigan of the ATGWU, for instance, became a founder member of the short-lived Socialist Labour Party. So did Noel Browne, although his anti-coalitionism was more nuancé, and although he actually flirted with the party (for however brief a period is uncertain) in the unlikely context of 1982. The anti-coalition stance of Pat Carroll, a former party vice-chairman, was in part an attempt to carve out a position distinct from the 'no coalition at any price' activists, but closer to them than to the 'coalition regardless of the price' view which is popularly ascribed to activists from the rural constituencies. Pat Carroll did not oppose coalition in principle but argued that Labour should at least wait until it had won enough seats to be the majority partner in such an arrangement: he left to take up a teaching position in East Africa which, although temporary, effectively removed him from the mainstream of anti-coalition politics within the party.

Trade union leaders, such as Billy Attley of the FWUI and John Carroll of the ITGWU, are not slow to make strongly anti-coalition noises between elections, but their vote at conference

11

has rarely been critical on this issue and, when it has, it has tended to be cast in favour of compromise solutions rather than in favour of an all-out ban on coalition arrangements.

In these circumstances, the leadership of the anti-coalition position within the party has to some extent been a shifting one. The 'Labour Left' group, which was founded in 1983 by people such as Brendan Halligan and Frank Buckley (a Labour councillor and former Dail candidate from Dublin South), is unashamedly anti-coalitionist, but professes a greater degree of loyalty to the party than, for instance, the Militant Tendency. Their loyalty appears to be recognised in the most unexpected quarters, in that they were given permission—for a short period—to hold the meetings of their group in the Labour Party's Head Office. It is a far cry from this to the controversial days of the early seventies, when the 'Liaison of the Left' group—which included Pat Carroll, Dermot Boucher (a subsequent migrant to the SLP) and other Left members of the party were more likely to be expelled from the party than offered the hospitality of its Head Office for their meetings. Where 'Labour Left' is different from its predecessor ginger groups on the Left of the party is not only, however, in terms of its standing, but in terms of its tactics. In the heady days of the 1973–77 Coalition, the Liaison of the Left prosecuted their cause with missionary zeal. The considered view of today's Labour Left is that the Labour ministers who took office in 1982 are doing all the anti-coalition group's work for them, in that they are making the concept and actuality of coalition so unpopular within the party that all the anti-coalitionists have to do is to wait for the party to 'fall into their lap'.

The most prominent—and permanent—opponent of coalition, and the most staunch advocate of further policy development within the party as a means of wooing the electorate, has been Michael D. Higgins. His position in the party has been chairman for a number of years now, but it would probably be true to say that it is also, partly, that of a mascot. Anti-coalition members of the party undoubtedly feel that as long as he remains chairman there is at least one good reason for staying in the party, despite their detestation of its willingness to participate in government. And there is no denying the fact that his skill in straddling the two horses of the party chairmanship and its anti-coalition wing (despite a few stumbles) is a feat of political bareback riding that

12

few have equalled. Likewise, pro-coalitionists, even if irked by his occasional stridency or by what they feel is an abuse of his position in favour of the anti-coalition cause, have never seriously entertained the prospect of putting up someone to challenge him for the chairmanship. They know that such a candidate would not win, or that at the very least it would be a bitter and divisive struggle, not least because both groups undeniably get a positive charge from the sight of their chairman in full oratorical flight, particularly on topics such as foreign affairs, in which he has taken an abiding interest, and on which (for, no doubt, obvious reasons) opinion within the party has rarely been divided.

Higgins, who shares with Noel Browne an impoverished childhood, initially joined Fianna Fail during a period when that party's radicalism was less suspect and when Labour, in the West of Ireland at any rate, was certainly not a force to be reckoned with and ideologically was as weak as it was politically. At the party's annual conference, where he will be rapturously applauded even by people who would be slow to vote for him in a contest, he makes the most of his chairman's address. The fact that his accent is a curious amalgam of phonemes from Clare, Galway, Dublin and academia in general is not a drawback. If anything, it seems to add to the fascination of his verbal flourishes as, sweating lightly under the arc-lights, he seems practically to levitate with the passion of his indictment of all that is wrong with Irish society. As conference chairman, he is required to be constantly on the alert; and he has learned the interplay, particularly with a crowded auditorium, to the point where there is almost a degree of intimacy about it as he extricates himself from some procedural error or from a momentary loss of good humour by puckishly throwing himself on his hearers' mercy. His political strength within the party comes partly from his obvious convictions, but also partly from his academic background as a sociologist, and from his insistence—which marks him off from a number of other equally left-wing but more 'liberal' members of the party—on the importance of economic issues.

Of late, however, it appears that his star may be waning: to have the doubtful privilege of being featured in *Phoenix* as a pillar of the establishment, with the none too covert suggestion that his radicalism is now more than a little threadbare, must indicate that some of his support, at least, is being eroded by the passage of

13

time. There is also evidence from his recent electoral career to suggest that anti-coalitionism per se is not a sufficient charm to ward off electoral disfavour, and that many other factors, not all of which have been adequately identified, operate in the electorate's collective mind. In the 1985 local elections in Galway, both Michael and the other Labour candidate combined failed to secure a quota. Michael had to wait until the seventh count to be elected, while his arch-rival, Workers' Party candidate Jimmy Brick, who had polled 20 per cent more votes than Michael and his running-mate together, was easily elected on the first count. This can be contrasted with the fortunes of a strong anti-coalition party member, Emmett Stagg, in the same local elections in County Kildare. Stagg, who did not take a running mate, secured 22 per cent of the first preference vote and actually brought in a Workers' Party candidate on his coat-tails.

For the time being, however, 'Michael D', as he is universally known, is probably the undisputed leader of that group within the party (although it does not operate as a ginger or pressure group as previous anti-coalition members have done) which sees coalition as the main reason for its recent run of electoral failures, and whose policy in general is summed up in the somewhat vague phrase, 'Socialist Opposition'.

A further group, of whom former leader Frank Cluskey is probably the archetype, argues that the loss of Labour support is not necessarily due to any shortage of policies, or to the fact that the party has gone into coalition, but has occurred because Labour, in coalition, has not been hard-headed enough about putting its case, and has effectively allowed itself to be led and said by Fine Gael on crunch issues which involve Labour credibility. It is hardly a novel point of view in the party: Young Jim Larkin, as Cluskey has reminded Labour's annual conference on more than one occasion, used to observe that the important thing about coalition was not whether you went in, but when and why you came out. It is advice that Cluskey himself has taken to the letter, resigning from the Coalition Cabinet in December 1983 on a point of principle, leaving (as *The Irish Times* said on the occasion) many dry eyes on the Fine Gael side of the house. As an analysis of the reasons for Labour's decline, it has its attractions, not least for those activists who are unhappy with the dogmatism to be seen on either side of the coalition argument, and who prefer to make

14

their own minds up on the issues as they arise. But it has the disadvantage that the remedy for decline is essentially a long-term one, in that it implies that all that the party can do is to send a tougher breed of minister into coalition cabinets. This process, given the composition and dynamics of the party as a whole and of the Parliamentary Labour Party as its Dail representative, would appear likely to be a protracted one.

The traditional complaint within the PLP about their Labour ministers, when in coalition, is that they become remote from the rank and file. In fact the ministers seem to follow a type of boomerang trajectory, in which they are furthest from their PLP colleagues in mid-term, and appear again on the horizon as the next election approaches. There are, occasionally, good reasons for this. In the 1973–77 PLP, for example, the Labour ministers could complain, as Brendan Corish did with feeling on one occasion, that the readiness of members to leak to the press made it impossible for ministers to be frank. At one meeting not long before the 1981 election, position papers on the economic situation were presented by virtually all PLP members, including some ministers: pithy extracts from all of them appeared verbatim in the following week's *Sunday Independent*. Ministers who wanted an excuse for reticence had been handed one on a plate. There is little doubt, however, that this was not the major consideration, and that the perception by Labour ministers of the obligations of collective Cabinet secrecy was, particularly during that coalition, of primary importance. Rigid adherence to this concept, however, (and it is a concept to which Fine Gael ministers have latterly paid scant attention when it suited them) poses the particular problem that the Labour faithful are not permitted to know how well (or indeed how badly) their representatives in Cabinet have been doing. This makes the evaluation of their performance all the more difficult.

Party members who are neutral on the coalition question, or favourably disposed towards it, will, naturally enough, be slow to blame coalition for the party's electoral reverses. The preferred explanation of these members—and they probably include the present party leader, Dick Spring—is that they are due to a weakness in organisation. It is certainly true that the complexity of the Labour Party's structure has never been matched by organisation of the professional sort achieved by Fianna Fail and

Fine Gael. And there is no necessary correlation between the gradual decline in Labour's national percentage share of the vote after 1969, and the number of branches registered at Head Office. In 1969 there were 501 branches, and this dropped steadily to 436 in 1972: but thereafter it began to climb again (with a slight hiccup in 1974): the total in 1977 stood at 549 and today it is 436. The number of branches in existence at any one time is not necessarily an accurate index of the effectiveness of any party's organisation (re-organisation to increase the efficiency of the party can actually reduce the number of branches), but it is at least a straw in the wind—and the 'poor organisation thesis' comes a little bit unstuck when one considers that since 1977 the graphs of party electoral support and party membership have apparently been moving in opposite directions. Again, some senior party people, such as former general secretary Colm O'Briain, make the point trenchantly that although organisation is essential for any political party, it is not an entity which can deliver political support independently of the other key elements in any party's make-up: its leadership, its policies, the performance of its members in the Dail and in local authorities, its public image, and so on.

Blaming the leadership is, of course, the last of the simple solutions advanced for Labour's haemorrhage of votes during the past fifteen years. Brendan Corish, however, was so universally liked in the party that any group of activists which sought to lay the blame on his shoulders—as Noel Browne found out—was inevitably reduced rapidly to the status of a small and querulous minority. Some party members—and none more than Mick O'Leary—felt unhappy with the working-class doggedness of Frank Cluskey's style, but he nonetheless inspired too much affection to be an easy target. Michael O'Leary had all the ingredients to make the Judas the party was evidently seeking: but like the original Judas, he went away and hanged himself, leaving something of a vacuum. One of his most bitter adversaries, Brendan Halligan, has described him, with a fine feeling for Graham Greene's phrase, as 'the whiskey priest of Irish politics'. There are some signs that the ground is being prepared for a similar exercise in blame apportionment aimed directly at Spring, despite the initial outbreak of comradely feeling in the party after his election: certainly a number of the votes at the Cork Conference in 1985, which went directly against his publicly stated position on the issue concerned, can and should be regarded by him as a substantial shot across the bows. His degree of control over the party is certainly closer to that of O'Leary than to that of Cluskey, with obvious dangers for his continuation as leader. What is less certain is whether any other leader chosen by the PLP would make the situation very much better.

———

Rather than look for large, straightforward, and simple explanations for such a complex set of events as Labour's loss of support has been, it is probably better to try, however tentatively, to apply a magnifying glass to the problem in an attempt to discern whether the problem is the same all over the country, where the Labour voters are going to, and what kind of people are most likely to vote for Labour—and against it.

One of the points that can be made about the loss of Labour votes is that it follows a different timetable in different parts of the country. Thus, the high point in terms of percentage share of the vote was in the Dublin region in 1969, when it reached 28.3 per cent—up almost 10 per cent on the figure for the previous election in 1965. The 1969 election was also the high point for the Connaught–Ulster region, although the figures involved were much lower and it is probably safe to assume that the growth was almost entirely due to the considerably larger number of Labour candidates in this area.

But if Labour supporters in Dublin look back to the halcyon days of 1969 with nostalgia, their country cousins have to look back a bit further—to 1965, in fact, when electoral support for Labour peaked in both Munster and the rest of Leinster, and was never to reach those levels (18.5 per cent and 19.2 per cent respectively) again. In 1965, indeed, the Leinster area had the highest percentage Labour vote of any area in the country, and the Dublin vote was no greater, in percentage terms, than that in Munster.

So, ignoring Connaught–Ulster for all practical purposes (although Michael D. Higgins' achievement in winning a Dail seat there in 1981 is certainly one for the history books), we find ourselves looking not at one but at two graphs for Labour support in the country as a whole. One graph—the 'country' one—rises and declines relatively smoothly: the Labour vote in Munster in 1981, for example, is almost identical to what it was in 1957. The 'Dublin' graph rises much more sharply, and to greater heights, and the fall, when it comes, is therefore much more catastrophic. The peak of the first graph is in 1965; the peak of the second is in 1969. Between 1969 and 1981 the Labour Party in Dublin lost more than sixteen percentage points of electoral support, more than twice the loss in Leinster (7.5 per cent) or in Munster (6.5 per cent) from their peaks in 1965.

The volatility of the Labour vote, therefore, is especially marked in Dublin. And when we talk about the loss of the Labour vote in the past, we are—with the exception of 1969 in Munster (whose significance will be discussed later)—talking about Dublin. This is why it is especially important to look at the Labour vote in Dublin, where the party had only one TD between 1957 and 1965, but rose to the dizzying heights of ten TDs in 1969, fell away to three in 1981, and in mid 1986 held four (Frank Cluskey, Barry Desmond, Ruairi Quinn and Mervyn Taylor).

There is some evidence to suggest that the most volatile Dublin voter is, typically, a working-class man or woman with inclinations which veer between Labour, Independent Labour, the Workers' Party, and Fianna Fail. The evidence is crude, but nonetheless interesting, because it offers at least a partial explanation for some of the things that have been occurring. Looking at the differences between the 1965 and 1969 general elections in Dublin, for instance, it is clear that the Fianna Fail first preference vote declined by some 8 per cent, whereas the Labour vote rose by just under 10 per cent. Significantly, neither independents nor Fine Gael increased their vote in Dublin in the same period. The vote for independent candidates and for Fine Gael candidates, in fact, fell by approximately 1 per cent in each case. Therefore, although it would be quite unsustainable to argue that the same individuals who voted Fianna Fail in 1965 all dutifully went out and voted Labour in 1969, there is at least some circumstantial evidence that many of them, together with a very small scattering of defectors from the ranks of Fine Gael and the independents, may have done so.

It is important, too, to look at another simple set of figures—the figures for those who voted for candidates outside the three main political parties. Traditionally, it seems, Labour may have been a reasonable alternative for many of these voters: certainly, in

18

Dublin at any rate, Labour has benefitted disproportionately from their transfers. If you were taking the standpoint of a political analyst in 1969 or even 1965, it would have been possible to argue that the era of the really small party and of the independent candidate was effectively over. Fine Gael had managed to absorb Clann na Talmhan. Clann na Poblachta had also been re-absorbed into mainstream politics, largely into Fianna Fail but partly, via the National Progressive Democrats (Noel Browne and Jack McQuillan), into Labour. Abstentionist Sinn Fein was hardly a political force any longer, its impact predictable and confined to certain traditionally Republican constituencies. All in all, it looked as if Irish politics was settling down into a nice, cosy pattern—not particularly cosy for Labour, perhaps, but at least offering it the chance of becoming the main focus of opposition to the two parties it has frequently lumped together as conservative.

Even by 1977, however, there were distinct signs that Labour in particular was being threatened by a re-growth of the splinter party. The vote for 'other' candidates in that election was exceptionally high at 7.3 per cent. It was to rise in the following election to 8.4 per cent. Discounting the intervention of Sinn Fein candidates in the 'hunger strike' election of 1981, it seems set fair to hover around the 7 per cent mark, and will undoubtedly jump with the addition of the Progressive Democrats. An opinion poll taken in July 1985 showed support for 'others' standing at 10 per cent and later polls put the Progressive Democrats figure as high as 19 per cent on its own. This is in dramatic contrast to the low figures for such candidates in the 1965 and 1969 elections, when they achieved only 2.9 per cent and 3.2 per cent respectively. High Labour votes, therefore, tend to coincide with low votes for candidates outside the three main parties, and a low profile by splinter groups.

Perhaps the biggest single effect of any splinter group on the Labour vote was in the 1977 election, which anti-coalition forces within the party generally depict as the inevitable fruits of joining Fine Gael in Government. At this remove, it is difficult to suppress a wry smile on reading one of the last circulars from Head Office to directors of election in the field, which stated categorically that, based on 'confidential' information, the Coalition was going to win the election! The post-mortem was more sober in tone.

'One key factor in the whole Dublin area', the official party report on that election read, 'was the intervention of "Independent Labour candidates" in Artane and Finglas. One of these candidates, Dr Browne, was successful in Artane, indicating that there was a Labour seat in the area. The activities of the independent candidates affected three Dublin constituencies directly; Artane, Finglas, and Rathmines West, where a selected candidate (David Neligan) publicly withdrew his candidature. But all the Dublin constituencies were affected, either directly or indirectly, by the establishment of an Independent Labour Campaign Committee which published an Election Manifesto and publicly campaigned against the Labour Party and its policies. This Committee conducted a vigorous, and at times virulent, campaign against the Labour Party, and unquestionably caused a lot of Labour voters to abstain or vote for other parties.'

For this and no doubt for other reasons, the showing of Labour in Dublin at that particular election was dismal in the extreme. Conor Cruise O'Brien lost his seat in Clontarf by 633 votes. He was someone who was accused—often unjustly—of neglecting constituency work, and a reputation, even an unjustified one, can tell against you. But in some cases he was beaten simply by superior footwork. One group of householders in his constituency, for example, had been promised local authority loans at advantageous rates of interest, but when the time came for the commitment to be honoured, the local authority had simply run out of money. After strenuous battles in Cabinet, it was agreed that a state subsidy should be given to the people concerned to bring their mortgages down to the level that they would otherwise have been. O'Brien did not hesitate to give the news to the secretary of the local residents' association: but the secretary concerned was one Dr Michael Woods, who, if the contemporary folklore was to be believed, had most of his family up for half the following night distributing newsletters with the good tidings around the district while Dr O'Brien slept the sleep of the just.

In Cabra, where David Thornley was beaten, his running-mate Pat Carroll missed the seat by a mere 138 votes. That particular contest was additionally marred by a squalid series of incidents in which High Court actions were threatened to challenge the right of certain branches to vote in the selection convention—a row at the epicentre of which stood the figure of Michael Mullen jnr, son

of the famous ITGWU leader, who was bidding to emulate ↑
own father's role in winning a seat for Labour in the same constituency. In Rathmines West, Mary Robinson, after a campaign
marred by bitter intra-constituency rivalry after she had been
added to the list of approved candidates by the AC, failed by only
406 votes. 'I could have handled it with more sensitivity at the
time', she was to say eight years later. 'I was unprepared for that
kind of faction in-fighting and perhaps I assumed my welcome
would be greater than it was. I took things for granted that I
should have worked harder at.'

Other candidates, like Justin Keating, were well beaten: a
celebrated photograph taken on the day of the count showed him
standing on a pavement outside the counting centre, hands in
pockets, the very picture of a man who had just been run over by
an electoral steamroller. Even Mervyn Taylor, whose seat four
years later in Tallaght was to look one of the safest for Labour in
the country, failed by almost 1,500 votes despite getting 20 per
cent of the first preferences. Overall, in that 1977 election, four
additional seats would have been won with the help of 2,001 extra
votes, judiciously spread around some of the constituencies
mentioned. Might-have-beens, however, do not cut much ice in
politics. Not long after the 1973 general election, when I had
scraped back into the Senate with a critical series of transfers from
lower candidates (at one stage the margin between me and
elimination was less than 100 votes) I met Keating in a restaurant
and we were comparing results. 'Every last vote and transfer may
be engraved on your soul until the day you die', he remarked
sagaciously, 'but as far as the punters are concerned there are only
two positions in politics. You're in—or you're out!'

Fifteen years on, the political landscape in Dublin is under-
going a transformation. This is because of the new-found electoral
significance of parties such as the Workers' Party, the Progressive
Democrats and Sinn Fein, organisations which are unlikely to
match the evanescent quality displayed by so many of the
colourful independents who surface from time to time, especially
at local elections. The proportion of people voting for 'other'
candidates is rising everywhere, but it is rising especially fast in
Dublin. In 1985, in fact, almost one Dublin voter in four went for
a candidate outside any of the three major parties, many of them
for Sinn Fein, whose electoral future in the Republic will probably

21

stently under-estimated by the media as it has been in
It is true that in local elections voters frequently vote
ndent or 'community' candidates in much greater
han at general elections: but the trends, particularly
Workers' Party and Sinn Fein in working-class areas,
Progressive Democrats elsewhere, are unmistakable.

If we focus on the Dublin Corporation area—Labour's traditional heartland, which has propelled people like Frank Cluskey,
Sean Dunne, John O'Connell, Michael O'Leary and others into
the Dail—the full extent of the disaster becomes more apparent.
The Workers' Party share of the vote was so close to Labour's that
it was, effectively, breathing down the larger party's neck; and even
Sinn Fein picked up almost half as many votes as did Labour.
When the question of seats is considered, the situation becomes
even more bleak: the Workers' Party, with about 1,000 fewer
votes than Labour, won six Corporation seats: Labour won only
two, bidding goodbye in the process to such long-time
Corporation members as Paddy Dunne (a former Lord Mayor),
Mick Collins, Billy Comiskey (another former Lord Mayor), Joe
Connolly, Diana Robertson (Deputy Lord Mayor in the out-
going Corporation), Brendan Byrne, Mary Freehill and Paddy
O'Mahony. Worse again, in many of the areas in which people like
these lost seats, they were also supplanted by either Sinn Fein or
Workers' Party candidates as highest placed losers, indicating that
the party had slipped not one, but two places in public esteem.

No matter how you look at it, it is clear that Labour in Dublin,
and especially in the Corporation area, is at the moment on a
hiding to nothing. The results of the 1985 local election,
combined with the results of the previous general election, mean
that in the traditional Corporation area Labour now has no TD
north of the Liffey, and no councillor south of it.

It can of course be argued that the area is of declining electoral
significance, as more and more people are located in the sprawling
suburbs, where the Labour vote held up somewhat better. This is
of course true to some extent. But for Labour to have to concede
effective defeat here does not bode well. And the defeat was
conceded, it can be pointed out, despite a strategy which was
designed to ensure that Labour polled more heavily in Dublin
than the Workers' Party. All the pre-election polls and soundings
had indicated that there was a very real possibility that the

Workers' Party would overtake Labour in the Corporation area. The campaign managers, fearful of the blow to the party's image if this happened, decided on a strategy of maximising the number of candidates in order to maximise the total number of votes. It worked—but with a savage boomerang effect involving the loss of six Labour seats. In a comment after that election, Barry Desmond took pride in the fact that Labour had out-polled the Workers' Party in the city, and put the poor result in terms of seats down to 'sheer mismanagement'. If mismanagement there was, the blame for it can as readily be placed on the shoulders of the party leadership as anywhere else. In a sense, it seems to have been a defensive return to the unthought-out 1969 policy of maximising the vote at any cost, even if it leads to a loss of seats. In an analysis prepared before the 1985 local government election, Brendan Halligan suggested that the party would be lucky—on the showing of the polls to date—to win four Corporation seats. As things turned out, even his tentative estimate was double the actual final result. And in the six years between 1979 and 1985 Labour's actual share of the Corporation vote has been halved. It is worth noting, before leaving the Corporation area, that the vote here was as low as 43 per cent in 1985 suggesting that this section of the urban working class was not so much leaderless as effectively disenfranchised.

Exactly who are the dwindling band of the Labour faithful in Dublin? The public opinion polls help us to identify them with some clarity and here, too, the writing on the wall is fairly readily seen. As might be expected, Labour's support is predominantly urban and working class. Even within this class, however, political support is now tending strongly towards Fianna Fail: pre-election polls in 1985 gave that party more than 60 per cent of the working-class vote, nearly four times the *combined* working-class support for Labour and the Workers' Party (at 8 per cent each). Those figures, and the actual election results themselves, underwrite graphically the possibility that a certain type of working-class voter tends to oscillate between Fianna Fail and Labour/Workers' Party. When times are hard, and Fianna Fail is in opposition, the strength and direction of that swing can be accentuated, and is perhaps to some degree uncontainable.

It is when one looks at the profile of Labour support by age group and by marital status, however, that the true dimensions of its electoral problem appear at their starkest. Labour support by age is a dramatic 'U'-shaped curve, high in the 18–24 age bracket and among those aged 65 and over, but so low as almost to reach disappearing point in between, particularly in the 35–49 age group, where according to the polls it was as low as 2 per cent in 1985. What characterises this age group, of course, is its economic status. It is the group which carries the greatest share of family responsibility, especially if its children are going through upper secondary or third level education, and its family burdens are therefore perceived most keenly. It is the group which is sharply affected by unemployment, by erosion of take-home pay, and by cut-backs in government services. It is also one of the groups which is most likely to turn out on election day to register its approval or—more likely—to express its disapproval, in terms of the political choices on offer. And it takes a great many old age pensioners or young voters to off-set the deleterious effects of a swing against the party in this critical area.

The problem emerges even more clearly when we look at Labour support by marital status. The rate of Labour support among married, widowed or separated people, at 4 per cent according to the 1985 opinion polls, is less than half its support among single people, which was then 9 per cent. If—and there are many 'ifs' about all of Labour's strategic options—the support of married people within the 35–64 age group could be brought up to the level of party support among single people, it would add another 2.5 per cent to Labour's national figures at a stroke. It is, of course, easier to talk about such strokes than to achieve them. Policies to remedy this group's grievances are among the most expensive on offer, which makes their introduction even more problematic.

The centrality of the argument that coalition is/is not responsible for Labour's electoral problems, and the passion of the arguments that it provokes and the personal hostilities that break out whenever it is under discussion, are perhaps not readily understood by many members of the electorate. If they are not inclined to vote Labour in the first place, they are probably inclined to view it as yet another example of Labour's propensity for internecine warfare.

There is one fundamental argument always going on beneath the surface. On one side of this argument are the people who believe that the party should, in theory at least, remain open in principle to the possibility of coalition, if the terms are right and if a sufficient number of Labour policies will be enacted. David Thornley plainly regarded himself as one of them when he argued strongly on one occasion that the people whom the Labour Party represents simply cannot wait for a Labour government, and deserve consideration now in terms of what the party can do for them in power, even in a minority role. Those on the other side of the argument—and they would include many who joined the party in the heady days of 1969 and left it in disillusionment or despair at some stage during the fifteen years that followed— believe that the good is the enemy of the best, and that Labour's urge to change a limited number of things in the short term is a fundamental obstacle to its satisfactorily changing everything in the long term.

The first point of view was spelt out in the four-page document which the AC submitted to the conference in Cork in 1970 at which the original 'no coalition' policy, which had been in force since 1957,. was reversed. 'By participating as a partner in Government', it suggested, 'Labour is aware that it cannot expect to secure all of its aims, but it believes that even their partial achievement will transform society for the better. Based on its progress as a party during the sixties Labour can confidently adopt a more flexible approach in its electoral strategy for the purpose of implementing its policies through legislation. . . . Labour's policies were not designed for permanent opposition but for implementation. To be a socialist is not to be condemned to perpetual opposition but rather is to be committed to achievement, wherever the opportunity arises to do so (sic), with honour.'

In the opposite corner, twelve years later, stood Michael D. Higgins, who in his address as chairman to the Galway Conference at which Michael O'Leary lost the vote on electoral strategy, did not mince his words.

'A case could be made', Higgins declared, 'for having a compassionate caring member of the Labour Party in charge of any of the areas where legislation affects the vulnerable, the poor or the unemployed. Better a caring person than an insensitive one. But surely in reply one could easily state that should this participation make it impossible to develop policies, one is merely offering a sop of compassion in place of a real political solidarity which should take the form of relentlessly exposing the roots of these problems.

The choice is not one of a little progress now versus a great deal of progress in the years to come. The real choice is between abandoning the critique, avoiding the harder opposition, adopting an enforced silence, taking what is allowed you, *and* making the case, developing the policies, organising for a genuine new society —Socialist society. . . . Of course fine people with compassion softened the blows of many an uncaring administration. They have sought to protect the vulnerable in our society since our party was founded. Today that is not enough.'

Depending on the way one looks at it, the recent series of debates about Labour's electoral strategy has either been a history of warfare punctuated by truces, or of truces punctuated by outbreaks of hostilities. A key mechanism in all of this has been the 'three-year rule' which, laid down by conference itself, dictates that matters decided on at conference may not be raised again for three years following the date on which they were first discussed. This rule is rigidly held to in respect of coalition debates, and treated with greater flexibility when other, less contentious matters come up for discussion. It ensures that there is not a bloodbath every year, but it also ensures that the bloodbath, when it comes, has three years' savagery built into it.

In retrospect, one of the most surprising things about the Cork decision in 1970 is not just that the electoral policy itself was reversed, but that a policy which was originally determined by conference was now to be withdrawn from conference completely. The particular AC resolution to which I have already referred noted that henceforth a decision on whether coalition was in the best interests of the party would be made by the leader and members of the PLP alone. Brendan Corish, in his speech, softened the centralist approach of this proposal by giving a personal commitment that Labour deputies would operate 'in consultation with the AC'. By 1979, however, when conference was held in Killarney, far fewer of the delegates would have been prepared to trust their parliamentary representatives to this degree, and what became known as the 'Cluskey compromise' became party policy. This formula, accepting the hostility of many delegates to coalition (and the suspicion of others) mandated the leadership to seek the approval of a special delegate conference for any proposal to join a government, and laid it down that such a conference should be held between the date of an election and the date on which the new Dail would meet. This proposal, by leaving the last word on the matter to the ordinary Labour activist, was enough to still the incipient anti-coalition rebellion. By the time Michael O'Leary came to the Galway Conference in 1981 as party leader, determined to wrest control of this vital aspect of the political agenda away from the rank and file membership, he was already too late. The Cluskey compromise, proposed by the former leader himself, effectively torpedoed two other policy initiatives. First, and most dramatically, it sank O'Leary's plan to have the decision made, not just by the PLP, but by a joint PLP–AC meeting, an assembly only tangentially less likely than the full PLP to come down in favour of coalition, as most delegates did not need to be told. This strategy also, however, negatived the anti-coalition position pure and simple—a position which would, if adopted, have left the party facing into the following general election with a strategy which would have been rhetorically attractive but politically highly ambiguous and not particularly well thought out.

The options, at special coalition conferences, are generally spelt out like this (the actual quotation is from the Gaiety Conference of 1981).

(1) That Conference endorses the report of the Party Leader on his negotiations with other political parties in Dail Eireann and mandates the PLP to vote in accordance with his recommendation.

(The Standing Orders Committee, in an addendum at this point, noted that if the above resolution were defeated, the following resolutions would be voted on in the order in which they appeared).

(2) Conference mandates the PLP to support participation in Government with Fine Gael.

(3) Conference mandates the PLP to support participation in Government with Fianna Fail.

(4) Conference mandates the PLP to support a minority Fine Gael Government.

(5) Conference mandates the PLP to support a minority Fianna Fail Government.

(6) Conference mandates the PLP to go into socialist opposition by nominating the Party Leader as Taoiseach, and voting for him and for no other nominee as Taoiseach.

Few votes are cast with as much enthusiasm, it is said, as those which are cast *against* something. It is therefore perhaps to be expected that the anti-coalition voters within the party, whose votes can be taken as roughly coterminous with the 'socialist opposition' alternative just mentioned, have not convincingly worked out the probable series of options facing the party's Dail deputies, however few in number, should such a strategy be adopted (i.e., option 6).

In a situation in which a single party or a group of parties have an overall Dail majority, of course, it does not much matter what the Labour Party's strategy is: the party is in opposition, making a virtue of necessity. Where the party holds the balance of power, however, quite a different situation would arise, and it is one in which not even the wording of a motion like this would be of very much practical help to the Labour parliamentary forces. Such a strategy, for example, would plainly prevent the Labour deputies from voting for anyone as Taoiseach other than their own party leader. It would not, however, bind them to vote against the nominees of all other parties. This might well be the interpretation put on it by certain party activists, but it is hardly the one likely to be most favoured by Labour parliamentarians. The reason for this is that, were the Labour Party in the Dail to exercise the balance of power by voting against the nominees of all other parties, the Dail would be unable to elect a Taoiseach—at least in the short term. The person who had been Taoiseach before the election would remain Taoiseach for the time being, and would presumably, in the absence of sufficient support for his or her re-nomination, feel constitutionally obliged to ask the President to dissolve the Dail immediately and prepare for a fresh general election.

Certain Labour activists—notably the Militants—not only fore-see but welcome such a result, and predict that the end result would be either a forced coalition of the two major parties as the price of avoiding an unnecessary election, or sweeping electoral gains for Labour should such an election become inevitable. Whether the electorate would see matters in quite the same light is, of course, debatable: and it is at least possible that they might be encouraged by the media (as they will certainly be encouraged by the two major parties) to put the blame for such an 'unnecessary' election on the small party whose 'stubbornness' had precipitated it. No matter what happened, it is certain that this course of action would provoke a constitutional crisis. The President has the

28

unfettered power, under the Constitution, to refuse a dissolution of the Dail. Should he do so, or at least postpone a decision, it is not difficult to see that enormous pressure would be brought on the members of the PLP to alter their stance. In such circumstances, the ambiguity of the conference resolution already quoted might well be of some assistance, because it would not prevent the PLP in the Dail from abstaining on the vote for the nominee of another party.

This possibility actually seems to have been foreseen in 1969, but the way in which it was approached was crabwise, to say the least. In the 'Canvassers' Notes' prepared for that election (and drafted by Brendan Halligan), the final question in a question-and-answer section designed to help canvassers deal with awkward queries read:

'Do you mean that Labour will leave the country without a government if nobody gets an overall majority?'

'The papers now admit' (the suggested answer ran) 'that the responsibility is on every party to form a government, not just on Labour if no party has a majority. Labour would dearly love to see Fianna Fail and Fine Gael coming together—that would be the real coalition in Irish politics. Anyway, Labour has never behaved irresponsibly in the Dail and we have supported progressive legislation whenever it was introduced. *On this occasion Labour will act with the full realisation of its responsibility to the people to see to it that there is a government*.' (Author's emphasis).

The problem about electoral strategy is in part that the hypotheses multiply in an almost uncontrollable fashion. If Labour is to declare for a hard-line socialist opposition position, in which it will vote against all other nominees for Taoiseach, and if the major parties are not provoked by this action into an unlikely unexpected coalition with each other, the ensuing election would be a high-risk area for all small parties. If Labour adopts a more modulated approach, it still has to face up to the need to help choose which of the larger parties it will allow to form a minority government, either by voting for it or by not voting against it. The 'socialist opposition' policy as drafted in the conference resolution would be to abstain: it could choose its moment to bring it down. A more flexible interpretation of the policy would leave Labour free to support a minority government of the second-largest party. This carries the undeniable risk that Labour

29

A more flexible interpretation of the policy would leave Labour free to support a minority government by voting for it, but without taking office. This carries the undeniable risk that Labour would be forced to continue to register its support for such a government whenever the other major opposition party decided to call a vote on an issue of confidence. The steely nerves that this would require over a period of, say, two years are not frequently found in parliamentarians of any hue. Supporting a minority government of the largest party, by simply abstaining, might seem in the circumstances to be the more attractive option. But it also tends to ignore the inescapable fact that any government in this situation will not be standing around like a flock of sheep waiting to be herded obediently into a corner by the Labour collies snapping at its heels, but will be planning for the moment when it can best wrong-foot the smaller parties and declare a general election at a time and on an issue of its own choosing, inviting the electorate to end uncertainty by giving it an overall majority. The history of minority governments in the past, with the exception of the short-lived Haughey government of 1981–82, suggests strongly that the Irish electorate responds in a somewhat predictable fashion to such an entreaty. In the immediate future, when the prospect of a hung Dáil has grown substantially with the arrival on the political scene of Mr Desmond O'Malley's Progressive Democrats, one thing above all is certain, and that is that the Labour Party, when deciding its electoral strategy, should at least consciously abandon the notion that it is operating in a political vacuum.

2

Follow my Leader

IN THE years since 1975, the Labour Party has devoured leaders and general secretaries with an appetite unequalled in any of the country's major political parties—four leaders and four general secretaries, to be precise. The mortality rate is due partly to electoral factors, but it is still above average by any standards: the replacement rate in Fianna Fail and Fine Gael during the same period has been just half of this. In any political party, such a turnover would be a cause for concern. In a party as small as Labour, it has undoubtedly been a major contributory factor to its public perception as a party of warring factions and political unreliability. In addition to the people who have held these posts at various times over the past decade or so, there have also been a number of strong political personalities within the party—Jimmy Tully, Barry Desmond and Conor Cruise O'Brien, to name the most obvious ones—who have contributed mightily in their own distinctive ways to the overall public image of the party, whether for good or ill. In a party as small as Labour, the personalities of people like these bulk unusually large, defeating the efforts of the political scientists to cram them into a grand theory of Irish socialism and providing the Irish electorate with many splendid diversions.

Brendan Corish's contribution in holding the party together during an exceptionally difficult period, and in taking a number of historic policy initiatives, is all too easily underrated. It is difficult to think of any other leader who could have survived the spectacular reversal of party policy on coalition in 1970, or who could have taken office in a coalition government after having promised to support coalition only from the back benches. In Corish's Labour Party, this provoked grumbles and, indeed, opposition. In the same party led by anyone else, it would have

31

provoked outright rebellion and, probably, a split.

Corish's background was hardly radical. He fitted in many ways into the traditional image of the rural—or at least non-metropolitan—Labour TD, and the occupant of an hereditary seat, at that. His father, Richard Corish, who had been a Labour TD for Wexford for many years, died in 1945, and given the pattern of Irish politics at the time (and since) it was virtually inevitable that his son Brendan, then a local government official, should have been chosen as the by-election candidate. Once elected, his seat was never in doubt until the 1981 election, when it seemed for a time as if he might be defeated. But leading up to that there had been a Dail career of almost three decades, including ministries in three different governments, and they were decades of particularly dramatic change, not only for the Labour Party, but for the society in which it operated.

His first entrance into the Dail in December 1945 had a touch of the Keir Hardie about it. He was dressed in a dark navy blue suit, and wore a brown muffler knotted around his throat. The proletarian overtones of this mode of dress were, it turned out, accidental. During the by-election campaign, he had been suffering from an increasingly aggravated throat complaint, which had finally necessitated an operation: this had actually kept him away from the election count, and for some time afterwards he was unable to wear a collar and tie. In a house in which sartorial standards were more conventional than they are today, the muffler was the only answer to his dilemma.

He served a long apprenticeship, but his general acceptability within the party—and no doubt his non-Dublin origins—were borne out when he was elected unanimously as its leader in 1960, following William Norton's resignation. He had by this time already served as parliamentary secretary to the Ministers for Finance and Local Government in the first inter-party government, and as Minister for Social Welfare in the second, three-party government of 1954–57. The twelve years of Fianna Fail government after 1960 would have taxed the leadership of a lesser man and, although he undoubtedly made mistakes during this period, the sense of continuity which he provided, and the experience which he gained, were always put unstintingly at the service of the party as a whole.

One of the psychologically low periods for his leadership came in the 1965–66 period. Corish had been pressed to accept a nomination for the presidential election in 1966. He would undoubtedly have done very respectably, but realised that the campaign would have been an exhausting journey up a political cul-de-sac. He was under no illusions, for example, about the nature and extent of the help he could have expected from the party's existing network of TDs, many of whom would undoubtedly have been slow to put any substantial, professional work into the thankless task of canvassing, organising public meetings, and getting out the vote. Like many decisions, this particular one had inescapable side-effects. The chief of these was that Labour, at a time when its visibility was increasing, was suddenly absent from a national election which might have been used to help focus support in the electorate at large. By not participating, Labour was actually saying something about its perception of the role of the Presidency, assigning it to an apolitical limbo. The other major parties seem to share this perception to a considerable degree, as subsequent events showed.

Shortly after this, Corish lost the services of Catherine McGuinness, now an independent TCD Senator, who performed Trojan work as the PLP's parliamentary officer, scrutinising legislation, writing briefs, and providing vital back-up for the leadership. Catherine's husband, Proinsias, had been expelled from the party in somewhat technicolour circumstances (he was accused of being behind an unofficial Labour newspaper which made no secret of its dissatisfaction with the PLP's performance) and Catherine had resigned on a point of principle.

His organisational team strengthened again by the recruitment, and eventual promotion to general secretary, of Brendan Halligan, Corish began to break new ground, both in terms of the move towards a more overt identification of the party with socialism, and in terms of the strengthening of its opposition to coalition. Nor was there a question here of a closet socialist waiting for the right moment to strike: there was a definable element of personal evolution in Corish's progress towards the positions he eventually espoused in the late sixties: he had, on one occasion, given a substantial hostage to fortune when he described himself as a Catholic first, an Irishman second, and a socialist third. This was to be thrown up against him on more than one occasion afterwards, even when it had ceased to be relevant. But

33

it undoubtedly was relevant for a while, and certainly helped to distance the party from a number of potential supporters whose socialism was totally committed to the separation of church and state.

It is important to recognise that Corish's initiatives were not universally welcomed, either within the PLP or within the party as a whole. His 1966 speech, in which he proclaimed socialism as his creed and that of the party, led immediately to a kind of euphoria. Speaker after speaker at that conference followed the Corish line by prefacing their remarks from the platform with the phrase 'Speaking as a socialist . . . ', as if they were caressing a shiny new toy, whose inner workings had not been, as yet, fully examined. But the fillip it gave to the party, not least in the media—excited by the 'student revolution' of that year and by the general sense of movement and unpredictability which characterised the sixties as a whole—was undeniable.

Announcing the party's conversion to socialism was one thing; leading it into a rejection of coalition, being quite specific, was something else again. The original coalition decision was taken in 1957, and had not been seriously questioned for over a decade. Nor, of course, had it ever been actually tested in the field: after each of the subsequent elections, Fianna Fail had been enabled to govern alone, either because they had an overall majority, or because they could count on the support of a number of independents. By 1969, however, the position was in some respects different. Not only had some of the original anti-coalitionists, such as Jimmy Tully, become increasingly disenchanted by the long and fruitless years in opposition, but some of the newer faces in the PLP were not as strenuously opposed to the idea of participation in government. At the Labour Party Conference in January of that year, Corish made his famous—or infamous, depending on your point of view—declaration that should a future conference decide democratically in favour of coalition, his 'continued support for socialism will be from the back benches'. What is less widely known is that Michael O'Leary, the proposer of the anti-coalition resolution, was so fearful that the motion would be lost that he pressed Corish to throw his personal weight behind it. Corish did, and his extempore reference to the fact that Labour did not exist to 'give the kiss of life to Fine Gael', made in response to O'Leary's private

34

plea to him on the platform, was part of an all-or-nothing attempt to ensure the passage of the resolution. O'Leary may well have misread the situation, and quite possibly it was not even necessary to bring Corish into the lists. Corish's intervention, however, was to haunt him for years afterwards, more specifically the following year when conference did a total about-turn on this particular policy. In the interim, of course, a number of significant events had occurred. One of them was the Fianna Fail arms scandal: the other, less publicly noticed at the time, was the death in a car crash in January 1970 of Gerry Sweetman, who as an unreconstructed conservative and Minister for Finance, had so dominated the second inter-party government as to give Corish a horror of entering again into such an arrangement.

There was also an impetus for a change in the policy area: in the 1954–57 inter-party government, Labour had had few clear or distinctive policies; its position at the Cabinet table was therefore considerably weakened. In the years between 1966 and 1970, however, it had put together a whole series of policy documents, drawn up by special committees and approved by conference. However unrealistic or short on significant detail some of these policies may have been, they were a conscious expression of the party's move towards a fully thought-out socialist position, and represented at least a substantial negotiating option.

It was Corish's good fortune, in part, that the 1967–69 period was something of a media honeymoon for the party. This was nowhere more true than in *The Irish Times*, whose political correspondent, Michael McInerney, responded with infectious enthusiasm to the prospect of the Labour Party advancing to power on the crest of a wave of popular support. Michael had been in his younger days a member of the Communist Party: but his later feelings towards the Labour Party were less the product of a desire to subvert the existing political leadership of Fianna Fail and Fine Gael than of an engagingly innocent and optimistic view of the nature of the Irish electorate and indeed of its political system. Donal Foley, a Waterford man who had been active in the British Labour Party when working in London during the war, and who was now News Editor of *The Irish Times*, was another supporter. With Mary Maher, he on one occasion wrote a brief for Corish (it is said in the upstairs restaurant of the Lord Edward in Christchurch Place) which was subsequently incorporated, almost unchanged, into the peroration of the Labour leader's famous 'New Republic' speech in 1967. One of the contributions by Donal Foley, whose father had stood for Labour in Waterford many years before, was the phrase describing Labour as 'the orchestration of dissent'. Foley subsequently wrote an editorial for *The Irish Times* (headed 'Orchestration of Dissent') praising Corish's speech! Later again, he wrote further editorials denouncing the Labour Party for its failure to live up to this image.

'Big Brendan', as he is still affectionately known, had a uniquely positive public image among supporters of all the major parties, but within his own party he had a number of difficult battles to wage and to win. One of them related to the appointment of ministers in a coalition government. In the first two inter-party governments in which he had served, the Labour Party had chosen its ministers by a vote of the PLP. Corish made it clear to the party that he would choose the ministers personally, and that if the party did not agree with his proposal, they could always choose a new leader. Some of his colleagues did not trouble to hide their disgruntlement when, in 1973, he exercised his new power with scant regard for at least some cherished traditions: Dan Spring, for example, who was only a few months short of the minimum period for eligibility for a ministerial pension after his service in the last inter-party government, was to see that elusive prize removed even further from his grasp when Corish decided not to appoint him.

It was on the question of the North, however, that Corish had to endure his most prolonged crisis, and his decision to appoint Conor Cruise O'Brien as Northern affairs spokesman, and to stand behind him in the face of fierce criticism from within the PLP and the party conference, helped to establish a policy line which, give or take a bit, has stood the test of time. On one occasion the PLP actually divided evenly on the question of whether or not O'Brien should remain as Northern spokesman, and when Corish, who had a casting vote, left the room to consider his position, there was near-consternation, during which Frank Cluskey was heard to remark that although all present would gladly consider themselves as candidates for the leadership should Corish resign, not one of them could find a seconder! On another occasion, a challenge to Corish mounted by John O'Connell fizzled out ingloriously. The meeting had been adjourned and reconvened: PLP members found themselves tripping over reporters in the corridors as they entered the meeting room, and there was a general presumption of imminent crisis. The crisis was defused, however, and in the mildest possible way, by Senator Fintan Kennedy of the ITGWU, who told the PLP meeting, in one of the shortest and most effective interventions ever made at that forum, that if Brendan Corish ceased to be leader then his union would have to reconsider its affiliation to the party. Corish participated in Sunningdale, and the spirit of that particular agreement was so firmly embedded in the party that when, in December 1985, a Militant-sponsored motion at the AC attempted to reject the recently-concluded Anglo-Irish agreement, it was overwhelmingly rejected. On the North, as Michael Gallagher has argued persuasively, the Labour Party has at least learned how to avoid losing votes, even if it has not mastered the art of winning them, and that this should be the case is largely a monument to Corish.

Politically and perhaps in other ways, Brendan Corish might almost be regarded as a late developer. His nudging of the party towards more socialist positions—on divorce and birth control, for example—represented initiatives such as one would not have expected from someone of his background. Conversely, it may well have been that it was precisely his background which enabled him to get the support of rural deputies in the PLP who were actually opposed to the points of view he was enunciating. A firebrand socialist from Dublin might not have done as well. One of his strengths, too, was a readiness to acknowledge his own limitations, and not to hesitate when it came to the question of recruiting people such as O'Brien, Keating and Thornley, who might be expected to outshine him intellectually. But he is no mean intellect himself, and would certainly be rated among the top four speakers in a Dail which included speakers as practised as Kevin Boland, Paddy McGilligan and others. He wrote all his own Dail speeches, often speaking from a sheaf of notes that could include as many as fifty or sixty separate points, and, during the 1969–73 period in particular, could hold his own in a Labour Party speaking team of exceptional brilliance.

Like his immediate successor, Frank Cluskey, Corish was a gifted amateur actor (and indeed a singer, too). Histrionics, however, contributed less to Cluskey's leadership than his early background in the trade union movement and (or so his enemies slyly suggested) his career as a butcher. The battle between Cluskey and Michael O'Leary for Corish's mantle had in fact been joined many years before, and was common gossip, although Barry Desmond would never have ruled himself out of the running. Corish was thought initially to favour O'Leary, but it became evident towards the end of his period as leader that the wary neutrality he adopted in public did not totally conceal the warmth of his feelings for Cluskey.

In the years prior to 1973, Frank's trajectory had been erratic, to say the least, with flashes of brilliance interspersed with periods of waywardness. After 1973, however, Cluskey had shown that the risk Corish had taken in appointing him as parliamentary secretary had been justified. O'Leary, as a minister, might be said to have had the edge, but in the final analysis the balance was so finely drawn that literally either of them could have succeeded. Ruairi Quinn and I, each of whom were to vote for Frank Cluskey in the leadership election, were treated to a brilliant personal canvass by O'Leary in an upstairs room in the Gresham Hotel, just after the election but before the change of government. O'Leary had been officiating as minister at a function downstairs, and Ruairi and I were summoned to the ministerial presence to be told, in a performance of sustained and intense lobbying power, where he felt the party was going wrong and where—particularly organisationally—it needed to be improved. Despite the fact that it rapidly became apparent that my personal commitment was elsewhere, the same canvass was carried out on an intermittent basis right up to the day of the election—in the Dail restaurant, on the stairs, or anywhere else we happened to meet. I have no doubt that other members of the PLP were similarly honoured.

The actual circumstances of Cluskey's election are detailed elsewhere in this book (cf. chapter 5), but the result, like all close calls, had a number of different effects, not all of them beneficial. O'Leary might well have thought that he would have had a better chance had a name been drawn out of a hat, as it should have been, strictly speaking. Or he could have felt cheated because the election was held while Sean Treacy was still Ceann Comhairle and therefore not entitled to attend the meeting and vote (in theory he could have resigned in order to do so, and the general presumption was that, had he been there, he would have voted for

O'Leary, giving the leadership to him by a margin of one vote on the first ballot).

The result may have had a different impact on both men. Cluskey, conscious of the fact that he had won by only one vote (and on a second ballot at that) may have spent the subsequent four years as leader with the need to maintain the unity of the PLP and the party as a whole uppermost in his mind. Party unity is, of course, an absolute essential for any leader—the bitter experience of the 1940s, when Labour split into its component parts, leaving 'National Labour' outside the fold for a number of years, bulks large in the consciousness of the labour movement as a whole. But in the case of the PLP between 1977 and 1981 this perceived need to strengthen relationships with people who had voted against him, and above all to avoid the kind of friction that might be caused by unilateral action as leader, led Cluskey to exercise a degree of caution that, with the benefit of hindsight, looks over-emphasised. It had its positive side: no policy initiative was taken without the prior agreement of the PLP or the AC, as the case might be; and a vote never went against him. For a while, indeed, everything went swimmingly, despite the grumbles from media commentators who would plainly have preferred the election of O'Leary as leader and who saw Cluskey as a gruff, uncommunicative, and conservative Labour leader of the old school. Those commentators were spectacularly wrong-footed by the European elections of 1979, which provided his leadership with a high point all the more notable for the fact that it was to some degree unexpected, even by Cluskey himself. When he walked into the upstairs lounge in a pub in Donnybrook on the night of the count for that election, the Labour election workers gathered there raised the roof—as well they might. But it was somewhat belated recognition for talents that had been to some degree masked by doggedness, and distorted by an unfavourable media image.

Born just off Dorset Street in 1930, Frank Cluskey left school early, and touched base in a number of unlikely areas (at one stage he had a job polishing milk-churns, at another he paraded greyhounds at a dog-track) before becoming an apprentice butcher at the age of sixteen. In the early 1960s his vote-getting activity, and his electoral energy, became something of a byword: he was elected a Labour member of Dublin Corporation in 1960,

and a TD in 1965, becoming Lord Mayor in 1968. When Brendan
Corish appointed him parliamentary Secretary for Social Welfare
in 1973, it was a job for which he was particularly well suited, and
a number of precedents were broken during the period of that
government when Corish brought him personally into Cabinet to
argue his case for social welfare expenditure. On at least one
occasion he threatened to resign: the Cabinet found the money,
and he stayed. The Combat Poverty programme, too, was a
substantial gain, and not only at European level, where the
Germans (for instance) had to be persuaded to help fund a
political initiative that would have caused them considerable
problems had it been implemented in their own country.
Domestically, it helped to energise a number of local com-
munities, and to challenge established ways of practising politics,
much to the discomfiture of some powerful interests who had
been prepared to tolerate it for as long as it operated like any other
'charitable' organisation.

What many people took as dourness was in fact the mien of the
poker-player and trade union negotiator: not even his closest
associates could ever be really sure about which cards, or even
how many, he held in his hand. But the public gruffness was
tempered by a humour, both in the Dail chamber and in private,
which could crackle with political electricity. On one occasion in
early 1986 he left a conversation he had been having with Garret
FitzGerald in Leinster House and sauntered over to a small knot
of Fine Gael ministers and aspirant ministers who had been
watching this somewhat unusual meeting.

FitzGerald, he told them, had decided that the voice of the
authentic Left was needed in the Cabinet, and had been discussing
bringing him back as minister.

'The thing is', he added, 'that our lads are doing such a good job
there I wouldn't replace any of them. So now he's got to decide
which of you he's going to sack . . . .'

The straight face with which this was delivered, and the
knowledge that he was a man who generally had to be taken
seriously, left even the most sceptical of his listeners with a
decidedly queasy feeling in the pit of their stomachs. There is a
striking parallel with a dodge that Cluskey, as an apprentice
butcher, had learned in the city abbatoir. The trick on a cold
winter's morning, when all the butchers were huddled around the

40

stove and there was no room for an outsider, was for anyone left out in the cold to beg temporary access to the stove on the pretext of lighting a cigarette, and—without being seen—quickly drop a loaded stun-gun cartridge inside. The resulting explosion would clear the area in a trice, and the miscreant could saunter up and take his place beside the source of heat at his ease.

Although he could be extraordinarily swift on his feet in the Dail, he rarely took snap decisions on policy matters, particularly on key initiatives like divorce or contraception, and there were times when PLP members like Mary Robinson, myself, or Ruairi Quinn would find the slowness of progress on these issues deeply frustrating. The lack of speed was even more galling on the two occasions when Noel Browne, seizing his opportunity—for once—with both hands, set out to embarrass Labour on the Haughey Contraception Bill and on the divorce issue. When, in 1981, Cluskey secured the agreement of the PLP for a motion on divorce which argued strongly that the question was not whether divorce should be allowed, but when, it was a notable triumph that only two of the waverers were absent—Coughlan and Spring. On the other hand, it could be argued that the victory was a Pyrrhic one, in that Browne—who was not even present in the Dail to vote for the Labour motion—had earlier stolen what little thunder Labour had managed to manufacture for itself.

Cluskey's caution, and his unwillingness to be rushed into taking up positions for which he was not fully prepared, had both its positive and its negative aspects. On the positive side, undoubtedly, was the fact that he was the only major party leader to refuse to give carte blanche to the abortion amendment proposal which was put to all the parties before the 1981 election. More questionably, that particular period was marked by a failure—for which all the TDs, and not him alone, must also be held partly responsible—to establish a sufficient distance between Labour and Fine Gael in the Dail. This can be seen most readily in the pattern of debates in private members' time, which Labour and Fine Gael shared on a week-about basis. The number of Labour Party private members' motions which Fine Gael were unable to support, and vice versa, was minimal. This was largely because most of the motions put forward by both parties were framed as straight-forward attacks on the Fianna Fail government, rather than as projections of the policy of the party concerned. In the case of both parties, too, there was probably an unspoken fear that putting too much of a gap between Labour and Fine Gael would have imperilled seats in the next election. There would inevitably be occasions—as in the debates on amendments to the Finance Bill, for example—when the two parties' attitudes clearly diverged dramatically. There were also undoubtedly instances in which, rather than vote with the government against a Fine Gael amendment, Labour deputies abstained, just as Fine Gael deputies did the same rather than vote against a Labour amendment. But they were few and far between, and generally ignored by the press, which was in any case coming to treat the opposition as a more or less homogenous block.

A classic example of this came with the Fianna Fail proposal to impose a 2 per cent farm levy in 1981. At a very poorly attended PLP meeting during the debate on this proposal, I argued strongly in favour of voting for the measure, Jimmy Tully against. Frank Cluskey maintained a keenly interested neutrality, but eventually came down against the proposal on the grounds—sacrosanct to Labour, after all—that it was a tax imposed without regard to the taxpayer's ability to pay. Subsequent developments—the youth levy, for instance—indicated that this principle was not as sacrosanct as had been previously supposed. During his period as leader, in fact, Cluskey did what he could to break away from the traditional stereotype of Labour support, and was genuinely interested in the plight of the small farmer, which he contrasted with the wealth of the average IFA member. The growth of the National Land League, around this time, was also being viewed as a potentially positive area for Labour among farming voters. Try as he (and various policy committees) might, however, the electoral support of groups like these continued to elude him and—again with the benefit of hindsight—it is possible to ask whether too much effort was put into unproductive areas like these at a time when the party had little enough energy to spare. A measure of the political hostility to these kind of initiatives can be readily gauged from an editorial in the Clonmel *Nationalist* at a time when the Coalition government in 1985 decided that it would introduce a land tax (15 June 1985). Describing the proposal as 'a dangerous flirtation with Marxist–Leninism', the editorial writer went on to argue that 'the land tax proposal may have its Communistic essence pathetically watered down—precisely the kind of legislative product one may expect when chalk and cheese indulge in the conceit of thinking they can together govern a country—but there is always the danger that some future administrations may progressively evaporate the water and proceed with the collectivisation of Irish agriculture.' Labour's effort to woo the farming vote, it is clear, smacks of masochism.

Cluskey's approach to the question of electoral strategy, as decided at the Killarney Conference in 1979 with the support of a substantial majority of the party, myself included, was his considered response to the difficulties of holding together the pro- and anti-coalition groups in the party, and in this he was aided considerably by a more uncommitted group in the centre of the party, including many trade unionists with whom he had particularly close personal ties, particularly in his own union, the FWUI.

It was an approach born at least in part of his trade union experience, of his desire to keep all the options open for as long as possible. It was evidence of the essentially democratic way in which he approached contentious questions, in that the party as a whole was to be given, via a special post-election conference, the right to decide on the PLP's Dail strategy. It also reflects a basic political unwillingness to surrender what might be valuable ammunition to an opponent. In particular, he was sensitive to the argument that Fianna Fail might make about the impossibility of forming a coalition (were Labour to oppose it) and the threat that this justifiable charge might pose to Labour's desire to hold the balance of power. His reasoning was simple enough: with all the options open, Labour's negotiating position was at its strongest. Ironically, he broke one of his own rules in this area in a radio interview during the Killarney Conference itself, when he was tempted by a reporter into suggesting that a wealth tax would be a pre-condition for Labour participation in any future government. At pre-election press conferences later this remark was to hang, albatross-like, around the neck of a man who had set his face against pre-conditions, and eventually it was submerged in a more general statement that Labour's policies on capital taxation were a vital part of its programme and would have to be taken seriously by any other party which wished to enter into negotiations about forming a government. The specific problem about this commitment was not that it would not have caused any difficulties for Cluskey, had he been leader after the election, but that the inevitable Fine Gael reaction before polling day would have encouraged voters in the belief that any alternative to Fianna Fail was out of the question, and perhaps led them to cast their votes accordingly. That, at any rate, is the way the argument ran at the time.

The loss of his own seat at the ensuing general election obscured the situation to some degree, for it could readily be argued that the strategy had worked: Labour had achieved the balance of power (more or less), and was in a position to negotiate. Perhaps the problem was that only half the strategy worked—that in order for it to have been fully successful, the subsequent negotiations should have been carried out by the man who had forged the policy, rather than by a new leader who had been plainly unhappy with it. There is also the objection—never easy to answer—that this particular strategy was in fact fundamentally a decision to postpone a strategy until after each election. And there is the final irony that Labour alone of all the parties in the Dail at the time (and since) is required, especially by the media, to have a policy on coalition.

Cluskey's electoral defeat was a particularly cruel blow, and came in the wake of a long drawn-out controversy involving Dr John O'Connell. After the constituencies had been re-drawn, it became evident that there was a substantial overlap between O'Connell's former Ballyfermot constituency and Cluskey's South-Central constituency. There were, effectively, only two options: either O'Connell and Cluskey would run in the same constituency or O'Connell would take half a step sideways and run in the constituency now known as Dublin West. O'Connell refused to move. Cluskey declined to oblige him by indicating willingness to run with him on the same ticket, and the impasse became the property of the Administrative Council. In the circumstances, their decision to avoid any potential danger to the party leader (as they saw it) led them to adopt the second option. O'Connell bit the bullet, resigned, fought in the same constituency as Cluskey, and Cluskey's seat disappeared. Some of Cluskey's friends argue that the wrong decision was taken on that occasion, but Frank himself was plainly not to be budged. The other side of the coin of his character is seen in his determination not to abandon any course he considered a matter of principle, even if the costs were personally high. When the controversy with O'Connell was at its height, in January 1981, he told a reporter, 'No-one, including myself, is indispensable to the Labour Party.'

The immediate post-election situation in 1981 was, therefore, one of considerable confusion, and when the PLP met, few doubted that the glittering prize, which had for so long eluded him, would be confided to Michael O'Leary's eager grasp at long last. And so it was—but it was not quite the fairy story it might have been, for all that it had been a long time in the making. Anyone who is politically involved is ambitious, and the party leadership is a reasonable objective for anyone actively involved. In O'Leary's case, that ambition and that objective had been combined for quite some time. After losing the leadership by only one vote, it became elevated to the status of an obsession which not only marked his deputy leadership period with resentment and disaffection, but seriously compromised his leadership when it eventually came about.

One autumn day in the late 1950s, in my first year in UCC, one of my fellow-students in the college restaurant pointed to a lantern-jawed figure, with a couple of days' growth of beard, seated at another table, dressed in a white roll-neck pullover and talking vigorously about Marx. 'That's Michael O'Leary', he said, as if no further explanation were needed. Nor, indeed, was it—and O'Leary's evident status as a dangerous revolutionary was enhanced by the rumour that the teacup from which he drank contained, on occasion, whiskey. Not long afterwards, as a delegate to a Labour Party Conference in the O'Lehane Hall in Cavendish Row in Dublin (this was before the days of the mega-conferences in Liberty Hall and other more capacious venues), he made such a fiery anti-establishment speech that the then party leader, William Norton, inquired sardonically (but *sotto voce*) about whether he had started shaving yet.

Like Barry Desmond, Michael O'Leary made the political pilgrimage from Cork to the upper echelons of the Labour Party through the channels provided by the trade union movement, and in particular the Irish Congress of Trade Unions. Before Frank Cluskey's star rose in the party, in fact, Barry was the colleague whose leadership ambitions O'Leary most feared. At one stage, the 1966 Commission on party organisation had begun to canvass ways of electing the party leader differently from the traditional election by the PLP, and in particular widening the franchise to have the party leader elected by the annual conference. On

45

hearing of this proposed initiative, O'Leary asked the then commission chairman, Niall Greene, 'What are you trying to do—have Barry Desmond elected as leader of the party?'

The gradual falling out of favour with Corish, and the loss of the leadership election in 1977, were blows which even his victory in the 1979 European election did little to assuage. Despite his position as deputy leader of the party, he was rarely seen at PLP meetings, at AC meetings, or at officers' meetings, which are in effect the 'executive' of the AC, and are attended by all the party officers, including the party financial secretary and general secretary. His appearances in the Dail became more and more sporadic, and after his election to Strasbourg he was rarely seen there. It has frequently been alleged, on his behalf, that during this period he was 'frozen out' by the Cluskey leadership and not allowed to play his full part in the party organisation. The fact remains, however, that as deputy leader of the party he chose to exercise his right to attend and contribute to all these organisations so infrequently that the goodwill which must have been there for him in substantial measure had virtually evaporated by 1981. On one occasion, after a particularly hostile, and anonymous, newspaper columnist had suggested that it was only a matter of time before he managed to unseat Cluskey as party leader, he had to be summoned to appear in person before a meeting of the PLP to be told unanimously by his colleagues that it was his responsibility to the party to deny such rumours explicitly if they continued to gain currency. It was a tense and unpleasant meeting at which his somewhat sullen defensiveness did little to win back any of the friends he had lost.

It might seem surprising, in the light of all this, that his subsequent election as party leader was unanimous, but in truth few people had the stomach to question it. It was an election by default, in a sense: given the leadership, O'Leary was now being invited to make good on the promise, and to live up to the expectations which had been so carefully cultivated over many years. There was, however, one condition imposed. As leader and Tanaiste, he would have to resign from the European Parliament, and Brendan Corish and other members of the PLP made it clear, at the meeting at which he was elected leader, that they wanted to ensure that this seat would go to former leader Frank Cluskey. O'Leary agreed. As the time came nearer for the first meeting of the Dail, however, and for the election of the new government, concern began to be expressed at the fact that the promised resignation had not materialised. Despite the virtual certainty that a coalition government headed by Dr FitzGerald would be the outcome of that first Dail meeting, it appeared as if the new party leader was anxious to hedge his bets. Feeling within the PLP— where Cluskey retained the strong affections of many—grew apace. Eventually, Barry Desmond confronted O'Leary in his office, and told him that if his signature to a letter of resignation was not forthcoming immediately, he would, as chief whip, summon an emergency PLP meeting to discuss the whole issue. O'Leary signed—but it was hardly an auspicious beginning to a leadership that was to end in dramatic circumstances such a short time later.

One of the ironies about that short-lived government was that the joint programme negotiated between O'Leary and FitzGerald showed evidence of rather more Labour input than did its successor, agreed between FitzGerald and Spring. The difficulties attendant on the implementation of even the FitzGerald/Spring programme, however, provided eloquent evidence of the difficulties that its predecessor would have encountered had the first of the two governments survived longer than it did.

While FitzGerald's first government was running into difficulties, however, O'Leary was also running into difficulties within his own party. The hard-line anti-coalitionists, while they might have been suspicious of Cluskey's strategy and motives, nevertheless respected him and knew him for a fighter who was difficult to put down. They knew that O'Leary was a committed coalition supporter, and they did not trust him. In the ensuing eighteen months, the leadership was to alienate the uncommitted centre group on the AC to such an extent that any of his proposals were viewed with automatic suspicion, if not with downright hostility. This process of mutual estrangement reached its apogee in the events surrounding the first 1982 election, when marathon all-night sittings of the AC were needed to hammer out a suitably ambiguous compromise—a compromise which O'Leary disowned almost before the ink on it was dry. The AC had to wait until after the election to take its revenge, but it then did so in no uncertain fashion, by effectively instructing the leadership not to enter a coalition—regardless of the fact that a new coalition was plainly not on the cards. There were some members of the PLP who thought that it might have been, and who regarded the AC action as a stab in the back. Barry Desmond evidently thought so, and got involved in an undignified public harangue with the AC chairman Michael D. Higgins about the propriety of the AC decision. O'Leary, for his part, decided to wait for the party conference in Galway, and there presented his formula which would undoubtedly have created a built-in majority for coalition in virtually any circumstances.

Shortly afterwards when O'Leary resigned as leader and, even before his successor could be elected, from the party itself. His subsequent decision to join Fine Gael came almost as an anti-climax, given all that had gone before. 'I had worked with Garret FitzGerald', he was to explain later. 'I shared many of his policy objectives; but the reason was that I believed the government then being led by Charles Haughey was not competent and that I would give any assistance I could to Garret FitzGerald in the formation of a new Government.' So far, so good, it seemed. It was not long, however, before he was accusing Fine Gael (and by extension FitzGerald) of conniving with Fianna Fail in a 'cynical consensus' to shelve the divorce issue. His subsequent attempt to bring a private members' bill into the Dail on the issue was fore-doomed to failure and was generally written off as a new-found enthusiasm: but it did at least have the effect of galvanising some members of his former party into putting down a bill of their own, without the support or even, it appears, the goodwill of their partners in government. His unaccustomed role as government backbencher plainly does not suit him; and he assumes that a Labour veto has been exercised to keep him out of the Cabinet. The fall-out from his divorce initiative, however, would probably have been sufficient to keep him out in any case.

When the PLP met to elect a successor to O'Leary, Cluskey took a decision not to contest the election, although had he decided to run it would have been difficult to defeat him. In the light of this, at least, subsequent media airings of suspicions that he was merely waiting in the wings to take over from Spring when the time was ripe seem previous, to say the least. But when it became clear that he was not standing, the battle lines were rapidly, and clearly drawn. Michael D. Higgins had declared his intention of putting his name forward, but it was not widely assumed that he stood much of a chance. Barry Desmond, on the other hand, might well have had more hope of success. The occasion which presented itself to him was not of the kind that is presented frequently, and he could not but be aware that if a younger person were elected, his chance of ever leading the party would be sharply reduced. For some time there was actually a doubt about Spring's candidature: his serious back injury, sustained while travelling in an official car during his period as Minister for State at the Department of Justice in the 1981–82 government, raised at least some questions about the wisdom of his contesting the position. By the time the meeting took place, however, the doubts had been cleared away, and although it was reasonably clear that he could expect the support of his fellow-TDs from Munster, this would not, of itself, have been enough to guarantee victory.

Three candidates were nominated—Barry Desmond (nominated by Frank Cluskey), Spring, and Michael D. Higgins (nominated by Mervyn Taylor). Before a vote was taken, however, it was decided to open a general discussion on the question of the leadership, and everyone spoke. One by one, the voices came out in favour of Spring, and when Eileen Desmond also signified her support, the practised tallymen around the table knew that it was all over. At this stage there was an adjournment, while Cluskey and Desmond conferred in another room. When they returned, Desmond announced that he was withdrawing from the contest, and some pressure was put on Michael D., unsuccessfully as might be expected, to follow suit. The vote, when it came, was a foregone conclusion, with Michael D. receiving the votes of himself and his proposer, and Spring receiving the remainder.

The total evaporation of the support he might have expected to receive from more of his colleagues must have been especially disheartening for Desmond. In fact, in less chaotic circumstances he might have stood a much better chance. But a number of factors, possibly including the imminence of the election and not least the geographical origin of the candidate concerned, led the PLP to prefer a candidate who had attracted no bad publicity (in contrast to Desmond), and who had the inestimable advantage of being young and photogenic. If they calculated that it would have a positive, shock effect on the electorate they were undoubtedly right: the result of the succeeding general election showed the first upward 'blip' in Labour Party national support in a general election since 1969 (the 1979 triumphs, of course, had been in the European election, not in a national one). During the election campaign Spring showed a toughness that belied both his years and his injury and—when he relaxed, which was all too rarely—a droll, mocking sense of humour which marked him totally apart in style from the other two party leaders.

Despite his youth, he might have been cast in the traditional mould of a Labour leader, but the son of Dan Spring, whose trade union background was always underpinned by a strong and traditional Republicanism, is not by any means totally defined by inherited characteristics. He has travelled widely, not least in the United States, where he met his wife; he has played international rugby; he is a qualified barrister; and the Kerry softness in his voice is overlain by a difficult-to-place intonation which owes something to Trinity College, something to the Bar, and something to Dublin itself. More than that, his political views are probably considerably more liberal than those of many of the TDs who voted for him in that leadership election. He has shown, on the divorce issue for instance, and on the constitutional amendment issue, that he is not afraid of making a stand that is electorally unpopular on his home ground in North Kerry (when a member of Tralee Urban District Council, it is said, he briefly achieved local notoriety by maintaining that a 'Hail Mary' should not be said during a meeting of that body). It could be said that he can afford to make gestures like this: in the November 1982 election he headed the poll in his own constituency, with almost 30 per cent of the first preference vote. A performance like that can stand a certain amount of attrition. But part of his problem may be that he is neither one thing nor the other: from Labour's rural hinterland, but expressing views that may find less than total acceptance in that very area; a moderniser by education and influence, but still far from accepted by the urban middle class—and especially the urban working class—voter. Part of his problem may also be that his rapid access to the second most senior political position in the country has sharply detracted from his potential appeal as a spokesman for opposition to establishment views and attitudes, which is one of the essential functions for any Labour leader. After one particularly trenchant speech in Cork attacking the banks, for instance, the ferocity of the banks' reaction stirred some nagging doubts among his advisers. They wondered, in particular, whether there was not a danger that he might not be taken seriously enough as a politician—that he might be accused of shooting from the hip too often. A tactical decision was probably taken on that occasion to increase the *gravitas* with which he appears before the electorate: but the price, in terms of a prematurely furrowed brow, may prove high in electoral terms if it is carried to too great a length. It is also unmistakably the case that he—or maybe his closest advisers—have been so affected by the unpopularity of the government of which he is Tanaiste that they tend to see conspiracies where none exist. Specifically, they fear the resurgence of Frank Cluskey as a rival, despite his decision not to stand for re-election as leader in late 1982, and a number of tactical decisions seem to have been taken on the basis of this assumption.

This was, for example, part of the backdrop to the extraordinary confusion about the appointment of a new general secretary to replace Colm O'Briain in late 1985 and early 1986. When the position was advertised in September 1985, the wording of the advertisement included one unprecedented paragraph:

'This very important post', it said, 'carries with it a rare opportunity to be part of the Labour Party's participation in the government of this country, and to contribute to it in a very special way.' The obvious decoding of this was that convinced anti-coalitionists need not apply. It is easy to understand, therefore the degree of confusion and upheaval generated when the man chosen by the interview panel for the post, FWUI official Bernard Browne, gave an unexpected interview to *The Sunday Tribune* before his appointment had been ratified by the AC. In this interview, he declared himself to be categorically anti-coalition. Almost simultaneously, his name had appeared on a circular from an ad-hoc trade union group, 'Trade Unionists for a United and Independent Ireland', criticising certain aspects of the Anglo-Irish Agreement which the government had only recently concluded with Mrs Thatcher's administration. In December, the AC meeting which would normally have ratified Mr Browne's selection without question divided sharply on the question, and decided not to make a decision, but to refer the matter back to the interview board and to the party officers. The interview board, as might be expected, said that they had no reason to change their recommendation, but the party officers—with the exception of Michael D. Higgins and Mervyn Taylor (chief whip)—decided in

January to oppose his nomination. At the time, it was an open secret inside the AC that some of the leadership group around Dick Spring believed—quite incorrectly—that Browne was going to be a dangerous ally, at the heart of the party organisation, of his fellow-FWUI member Frank Cluskey.

The turbulence surrounding Browne's nomination was hardly unprecedented. Since Brendan Halligan took up the position in 1968, in fact, it is a role which has attracted its share of controversy and, in Halligan's case, that controversy was frequently connected with his acknowledged electoral ambitions. Appointed to the Seanad by the Coalition in 1973, he had actually been cultivating a Northside constituency when he was hi-jacked into the Ballyfermot by-election in 1976. He served out the remainder of that period of government in the Dail, becoming increasingly frustrated at the limitations placed on government backbenchers: if he made a speech, for example, that was mildly critical of government economic policy, the heat of media attention (and the political attention of his annoyed colleagues) was rapidly turned on him, giving him a degree of personal publicity that he found somewhat double-edged. It rapidly became obvious that his original ambitions to fight for a seat in Finglas had not by any means been altered by his temporary transfer to Ballyfermot, but his forays into that territory were increasingly fruitless. After collecting just under half a quota in the 1977 election, he was beaten for the last seat by Luke Belton of Fine Gael by some 900 votes. Despite (or perhaps because of) the help of a devoted election team, quite a few of whom came from outside the constituency, Halligan never managed to overcome the distrust and even the hostility of the local Labour organisation. He had to take a Labour running-mate with him on the ticket, even though the logistics of the situation indicated that a single candidature would have been preferable, and his campaign was further thwarted by the intervention of former Labour man Matt Merrigan.

The irony of the situation was that, even in these circumstances, Halligan polled more than twice as many votes as the Workers' Party Proinsias de Rossa, who was later to take the seat. By 1981, Halligan's vote had been almost exactly halved, and de Rossa had overtaken him. 1977, therefore, represented the high point of his electoral career: thereafter it was downhill, aided and abetted by a marked public abandonment of previously-held positions, notably on coalition. Prior to 1970, he had been strongly in support of the party's anti-coalition strategy. Afterwards, he described coalition as 'an eminently sensible, intelligent and practical way of putting your policies into practice'. A decade later, his views had reverted to the original pattern, and his relationship with the party leadership after the 1981 election became completely soured. Michael O'Leary even at one stage tried to bring pressure to bear on Euro-TDs Seamus Pattison and Sean Treacy to abrogate an agreement they had with Halligan under which he did research work for them.

His re-dedication to anti-coalitionism (he says now that he regretted 'changing feet' on coalition in 1970) helped to secure him a party nomination to the European Parliament, with Flor O'Mahony, after Seamus Pattison and I resigned in late 1982. As general secretary he had been a particular object of suspicion among anti-coalitionists after 1970, more especially for his unwillingness to risk party division by challenging conservative barons such as Michael Pat Murphy and Stevie Coughlan, but he rapidly became active (but only for a time) in the publication of *Labour Left*, published by the broad, non-Militant anti-coalition group in the party, in which journal he made the extraordinary prediction that he would lose his own seat. His reputation was further damaged, however, by an apparent indecisiveness evidenced by his decision to pull out of the electoral race in Finglas in the first 1982 election after having been selected as an official Labour candidate, and repeating this performance in the European elections two years later. Nor was his credibility enhanced later when (in April 1985) he argued publicly for a 'grand coalition' which would rule for fifteen years, and criticised by implication the present PR system (in private he has been an advocate of the continental type 'list' system for Irish elections). Whatever else it was for, it was certainly not for this that he was appointed chairman of Bord na Mona in July of the same year. His gifts for analysis lacked a sounder sense of strategy, and were frequently derailed by a political waywardness that not even his closest associates professed to understand. It is in the area which first propelled him into politics—the growth of the cooperative movement and worker participation in industry—that he may yet make an important contribution to the development of socialist thinking in Ireland.

The interregnum after his resignation lasted for quite some time until Seamus Scally, the assistant general secretary, took his place on the nomination of Jimmy Tully at the AC. Seamus, whose Roscommon origins marked him off from both his predecessor and his successor, maintained an extremely low profile as general secretary and ended up, after resigning from this position and via a spell in Richard Burke's *cabinet* in Brussels, working with Liam Kavanagh as Minister for the Environment.

With the appointment of Colm O'Briain as Scally's successor, however, the fire was rapidly stoked for further controversy. O'Briain, who had been director of the Arts Council for eight years and a Labour supporter of long standing, is a mercurial, to some degree iconoclastic figure who plunged into the task of re-organising and galvanising the party with an energy that few expected, and that some did not welcome. In a moment of exasperation, he once referred to the problems caused by the existence of unnamed 'personal fiefdoms' within the party, and it was obvious that the resistance, especially in some rural constituencies, to the activities of an innovative (read 'interfering') general secretary, both in organisational and financial terms, was ultimately critical. So was the growing estrangement between O'Briain and his party leader, Dick Spring, the roots of which have never been explained. It is enough to indicate that the media's source for the information that O'Briain had tendered his resignation in June 1985 was close to the party leadership, and that Spring himself conspicuously made no attempt to get him to change his mind. A lack of trust at that level would plainly have made O'Briain's position untenable before long, even if the resistance of the rural fiefdoms had not. His departure, if it did nothing else, signalled a dramatic end to what had been a courageous initiative aimed at least in part at winning back urban liberals from their allegiance to FitzGerald's Fine Gael, and forging an essential link with them as part of the attempt to build up a renewed and professional party.

The appointment in January 1986 of Ray Kavanagh as O'Briain's successor marked the growing *impasse* between Spring and some members of the AC in a particularly acute way. The Spring group would not accept Browne after his gaffe. Another strong minority on the AC could not accept Fergus Finlay, who as Spring's personal representative in the Government Information Service might be expected to have the full confidence of the leader; and a compromise appointment seemed to be the inevitable outcome.

There are three other people who have been publicly associated with the Labour Party for a decade or longer, and who have become as familiar household names—although for different reasons—as the people who have led their party. One of them is undoubtedly Jimmy Tully. In recent memory, he is generally credited with having been one of the most powerful rural political barons, and an able, if conservative, Minister for the Environment, in the 1973–77 Coalition government. Reading further back in the history of the party, however, one is struck by the frequency with which his name crops up in the fifties and early sixties, not least as party chairman. The role was not as public a one then as it is now—indeed the holder of the post was known for many years only as chairman of the AC, and not as chairman of the party—but it nevertheless involved a substantial amount of organisational responsibility. Tully's name crops up in committee after committee, and it is clear that he more than played his part in giving the party whatever sense of cohesion and energy it had at that time. Less well known too, perhaps, is his history as general secretary of the Federation of Rural Workers, which later amalgamated with the Workers' Union of Ireland to form the FWUI. The almost total disappearance of the rural worker from the social and political landscape should not be allowed to obscure the fact that this particular worker was, traditionally, one of the most exploited in the country: and Tully's rural origins and sensibilities were always tempered by his background in this area. He would fight within the PLP, using whatever weapons came to hand, for his generally conservative point of view, but it was a point of honour with him to obey the collective decision afterwards, and not to break ranks in public even if the decision had gone against him, as it increasingly did in the seventies. And he was probably unique among the conservative members of that PLP in supporting the Labour Party motion on divorce in the Dail in 1981 out of conviction, based on his personal knowledge of the hardship caused by the present ban. Others, like John Ryan and Sean Treacy, had to be cajoled or bullied into supporting it: those who could neither be bullied nor cajoled stayed away. Cluskey, during his period as leader, was not afraid to oppose Tully when he felt it necessary: but equally he regarded Tully as a sort of litmus test for whatever course of action he happened to be proposing. If Tully was on-side, or at least neutral, the other conservatives posed less of a problem. It was partly because of his self-imposed silence

55

when decisions went against him that Tully could be ruthless in his denunciation, within the PLP, of those of its members who continued to wage their battles outside the door after losing them inside. Michael D. Higgins, myself and Mary Robinson were among the sinners in this regard, as might be expected.

Barry Desmond, a more complex character by any standards, is plainly one of the Labour Party's great survivors, holding on to the Dun Laoghaire seat which he carved out in 1969 with the tenacity of a water-buffalo unwilling to be separated from his favourite patch of pampas grass. He was unlucky not to have been given a Cabinet post in the 1981 Coalition government—or perhaps it was inevitable, in the light of the coolness between him and O'Leary. But he made his position as junior minister in the Department of Finance into a platform from which he achieved, very rapidly, fully ministerial levels of public prominence. Later, as Minister for Health and Social Welfare, he set about attacking waste in the system with a single-mindedness that alarmed Labour defenders of public expenditure almost without exception. At the same time, however, he was taking genuine initiatives on contraception (the 1984 Family Planning Bill, passed despite the vocal, if uncoordinated, opposition of the Catholic hierarchy, marked something of a turning point in Irish politics), adoption, and other social matters. His leadership ambitions may have been quenched by Spring's election, but never is a long time in politics, and the volatility of the system, and of the parties, may yet give him his chance.

If Desmond is a man who has earned his share of unpopularity, both inside and outside his own party, he has never scaled the peaks achieved by Conor Cruise O'Brien. During his period in active politics between 1969 and 1978, O'Brien became almost a national symbol, idolised and reviled in proportions that were always difficult to establish. He became synonymous, for example, with the strongly anti-IRA policy adopted by Labour against the vigorous opposition of people like Sean Treacy, despite the fact that this policy had been largely pioneered by Cluskey and O'Leary. His enemies labelled him as not only anti-IRA, but anti-Republican, an enemy of the Constitution itself, and as Minister for Posts and Telegraphs his appetite for attacking the IRA and those whom he perceived as their fellow-travellers grew apace, to the point where it became an obsession difficult to understand

56

from the outside. Like all government ministers during this period, his home and family were subjected to continuous threat, usually by anonymous telephone callers, to a degree that would possibly have broken people of less strength.

If one of Conor's notable characteristics was his ability to achieve levels of publicity almost effortlessly, his political indiscretions never extended to questions relating to Cabinet. Some of those who knew him, and many of those who did not, assumed that the end of his period of office would inevitably be marked by a book in which all would be revealed. This did not happen, and it is quite probable that the bonding experience of that particular Cabinet, under such threats and pressure from the sponsors of illegal violence, must have been very strong, even between people who were ideologically quite distinct from each other. Rejection of IRA violence, indeed, was a powerful cement. One wonders what some of his Cabinet colleagues must have made, in the circumstances, of one of his idiosyncrasies at PLP meetings. This was to rotate a biro rapidly between finger and thumb. This habit, unexceptional in itself, has the odd side-effect of producing a noise rather like that of small-arms fire in the distance. The intensity of the fusillade was a fairly accurate guide to his degree of agitation about the issue under discussion, and, as the moment for his intervention in the debate arrived, it would reach a positive crescendo.

Despite many of his critics' best efforts, he could never be completely type-cast: he was indefatigable in his support for units of the party organisation, no matter how insignificant, and cheerfully gave up his time to travel to meetings in areas in which Labour votes, let alone Labour seats, were something of a rarity. His enthusiasm for coalition was dominated by his undoubtedly passionate opposition to Charles Haughey, and the two fed off each other, in political terms, to an extraordinary extent. I suspect that the balance of the battle favoured Haughey; certainly O'Brien served to maximise the Fianna Fail vote, rather than to reinforce that for his own party or even for Fine Gael. Not that this deterred him. He was not afraid, for example, to carry his views even into the farthest west, where he was once seen (during the by-election campaign which elected Enda Kenny) in a pub wearing a white linen suit and looking for all the world, as one observer put it, like a tea-planter with amnesia. It is a pity that his published works are not likely to include a selection of the letters he wrote while minister—notably those to party colleagues like Frank Cluskey, Michael O'Leary, and Brendan Halligan. They rarely agreed with him and even less frequently took the advice he dispensed with a quixotic, and some would say arrogant, disregard for the consequences.

His departure from active politics, when it came, had little of the panache with which he had enlivened the scene. As a Senator, he was relieved of his role as Northern spokesman by Cluskey: eventually he resigned his Senate seat—more honourably than many others—when he reckoned that he simply could not give the time to it as well as exercising editorial responsibilities at *The Observer* in London. Later, he was to tell an American audience that he had been glad to leave representative politics because he had had to say so many things in which he did not believe, and when he wrote to resign his membership from the party on account of the Anglo-Irish agreement it was discovered that it had by that time already lapsed.

The pressures of clientelism, perhaps also of government, and undoubtedly of recession, have combined to ensure that today's Labour Party, however well endowed in other areas, seems somewhat the poorer for the absence of such personalities.

3

Rebels and Outcasts

BACKBENCHER, as *The Irish Times* columnist John Healy was then known, alerted his readers in January 1967 to a new feature in Irish politics. 'There are, outside of Parliament,' he wrote 'young intellectuals who know all the faults of the Parliamentary (Labour) Party, who know how to go about making it a party, what it needs as a fighting party. But when it comes to the nutcracker stage at election time, they prefer to sit on their intellectual fences, giving their advice privately and from afar, carefully foregoing the distasteful experience of submitting themselves to the electorate.'

The people to whom he was referring hardly needed his words to galvanise them into electoral activity. The stage had already been set by Brendan Corish's speech to the party's 1966 Conference, in which he proclaimed a public allegiance to socialism for the first time, and was to be further strengthened by his 1967 'New Republic' speech, in which he hammered the point home. The three most prominent of the people to whom he was undoubtedly referring—Conor Cruise O'Brien, Justin Keating and David Thornley—were to make their own allegiance more public very shortly, and all were elected to the Dail in 1969 on a wave of public opinion that was at least as much anti-Fianna Fail as it was pro-Labour or pro-anything. Only one of these became a party 'rebel' in the generally accepted sense of the word. What is more important to recognize, however, is that their advent to the party, and to the Dail, set up tensions which were to ensure that from then on there would be at least two species of rebels in the party. The traditional rebels on the Left, of whom Noel Browne is perhaps the archetypal example, were complemented by rebels on the Right, previously secure in their political near-independence, but now goaded by what they regarded as the pretensions of the 'intellectuals', and the threat to their electoral prospects represented by all the talk of socialism and its related dangers.

It is difficult to identify an archetypal right-wing Labour Party rebel, as they form a relatively homogenous group. What is certain is that the tensions between them and the newcomers created such friction within the PLP that during the 1969–73 Dail meetings of that grouping were more volatile than at any time before or since.

Their commonality resided in part in a hawkish stance on Republican issues, trenchant conservatism on social issues, and a strong pro-coalition stance, conditioned no doubt in part by the sixteen barren years of parliamentary opposition which their left-wing adversaries within the party had not shared. They can be distinguished from other Labour conservatives, such as Jimmy Tully, by their willingness to buck the party line more or less whenever it suited them. They tended to come from west of a line drawn roughly between Galway and Waterford, and Stevie Coughlan, if not archetypal, was certainly one of the most colourful of them.

Coughlan first achieved political prominence in his native city of Limerick as a member of Clann na Poblachta, which was originally formed in 1946 with strong Republican backing after two IRA men had been executed in Britain. It attracted many Fianna Fail activists, impatient at their party's record on the North and suspicious of its slow decline into social conservatism after the social democratic initiatives of the 1930s. Fianna Fail actually at one stage accused it of Communistic tendencies which, given Coughlan's later record, is more than a little absurd—but it was also, for a time, the party of Noel Browne and of other people who found a home, if that is the right word, on the left wing of the Labour Party.

Clann na Poblachta was formally dissolved in 1965, but Coughlan was by that stage already a member of Labour, having joined in 1961. He was elected as a Labour TD in 1965 and assumed the hardly onerous responsibilities in the Dail of spokesman on the Board of Works. Given the number of pies in which that particular department has its fingers, however, it undoubtedly suited Coughlan, a politician of the old clientelist school. No sooner had the election taken place in 1969, however, than Coughlan was in the wars with the new boys, his first public brush coming after Barry Desmond, hardly one of the 'intellectuals' to whom John Healy had referred but far enough to the Left to be anathema to Coughlan, had tweaked the Limerick deputy's nose by parading in protest outside a rugby match involving a South African team in Limerick—a match which Coughlan made a point of attending. It is worth noting in passing that rugby, in Limerick, is much more a working-class sport than it is in many other areas of Ireland, and Coughlan's attendance, whatever else he may be accused of, could hardly be classed as social climbing. Coughlan responded to the insult in typical fashion. 'What a cheek', he fulminated, 'for this jumped-up, overnight politician to come here to Limerick to tell us how we should act!'

Emboldened, perhaps, by Desmond's initiative, some of Coughlan's own natives became restless, touching off a series of internal conflicts in the Limerick organisation of the party which tended to centre around one branch in particular, that for St Mary's Abbey. A spokesman for this branch at the same time described their own TD's attitude to the party as 'that of a feudal lord' which, in the circumstances, was probably not an understatement. Attempts by others in the party to apply some discipline from above were met with equally spirited rebuffs. In 1970, for example, he greeted a critical speech by Conor Cruise O'Brien with the flat statement that 'I am not going to be disciplined by these newcomers to the party'.

By now, however, Conor Cruise O'Brien was not the only cross that Stevie Coughlan had to bear. The influx of activists into the party were frequently appalled by some of his statements and actions, and a hint of things to come was provided in the same year when a group of Irish Maoists (a forgotten breed of mostly student agitators whose direct action techniques made them something of a political nine days' wonder at the time) opened a bookshop in Limerick the better to propagate their gospel. After an unknown Limerick defender of the faith had discharged a gun at these premises, ordinary Labour Party members were horrified, for all that they did not share the views of the small group of Maoists. Their anger, however, was rapidly turned on Coughlan when, instead of condemning the outrage, he took a potent, sideways swipe at the victims. 'Any fellow with one eye open and the other closed', he averred stoutly, 'could see this coming. I am

61

vehemently opposed to these people.'

The matter was not allowed to rest there by left-wing (and indeed by many Centre) members of the party, but Coughlan refused to recant, and indeed this was not the only offence he had given. In another speech around the same time, dealing with historical aspects of the Jewish commercial presence in Limerick (a city from which they had been expelled forcibly in the early years of this century after a number of inflammatory sermons by a local priest) Coughlan used the words 'bloodsuckers' and 'extortionists' The impact on rank and file members of the party can be imagined. This time, an apology was inescapable, and it was tendered less than a week before a critical PLP meeting at which a bitter debate would undoubtedly have taken place, followed by the removal of the whip. Brendan Corish, not for the first time or the last in a difficult position in relation to party discipline, repudiated the speech and the sentiments it had contained, and there the matter was allowed to rest. The rumblings within the party as a whole, however, never completely subsided, and feelings were therefore quickly aroused later when a similarly injudicious remark set the party, and the press, alight.

By now the AC wanted to expel him, not just from the PLP but from the party itself. The manoeuvrings within that body were hectic, and there were threats of counter-expulsions, one coming from David Thornley, who had formed a *mésalliance*, inexplicable to many of his associates, with the Limerick deputy, and who threatened to put down a motion to expel Noel Browne if the motion calling for Coughlan's expulsion succeeded. It was not difficult to sympathise with Brendan Corish's position, or with the sombre assessment of the political correspondent of *The Irish Times* that 'so many independent points of view have been uttered recently by Labour Party deputies that it will be extremely difficult indeed for Mr Corish to take action against everybody' (7 April 1972).

Like the US Fifth Cavalry, Coughlan again came charging to his own rescue, issuing in Limerick an extraordinary speech—extraordinary, that is, in the light of his record—in which he called for a new Ireland under a secular, liberal constitution. 'Never before', muttered the same political correspondent in evident disbelief, 'have such sentiments been uttered by Mr Coughlan'. Nor were they to be again. Coughlan's star was already on the wane in Limerick. Mick Lipper, who had proposed Coughlan for the

Mayoralty successfully in June 1969, was chosen as a by-election candidate in February 1973 and, after an astonishing showing, secured the backing of many anti-Coughlan elements in the party organisation in the city. He ran and was elected as an independent in 1977, effectively taking Coughlan's seat, with the blessing of the same bishop who had—through Coughlan—sent a message of greeting to the party when it had staged its annual conference in Limerick!

Such was the relief in the PLP that Lipper was welcomed back into the fold with what Coughlan would have plainly regarded as indecent haste. In April 1979, two years after they had last appeared at a Labour Party Conference, both he and his son, whom many people supposed he had been grooming in the dynastic tradition, announced formally that they were severing their connections with the Labour Party. As a Parthian shot, Stevie announced that he was writing his memoirs.

It is important to spend some time on Stevie Coughlan, not only because he is a fair representative of the right-wing rebels in the Labour Party, but because the contrast between him and the man who is generally regarded as having been the archetypal left-wing rebel—Noel Browne—could not be more marked. Indeed, they were in some way entangled with each other, even though—or perhaps because—they stood at opposite ends of the party spectrum. Coughlan did everything but actually name Browne in a speech in Cork in 1971 when he maintained that two years previously the Labour Party had 'put it on the plate' for Fianna Fail in part because they had put up as a candidate 'a man who was absolutely opposed to everything that was Christian and Irish!' The differences between the two men were markedly physical as well as ideological. Coughlan, a round-shouldered bull of a man with a face like the rising sun and a voice trained in the hardest school of all—the bookmakers' pitch—went into combat at PLP meetings with a relentless single-mindedness that could wear down all but his most persistent critics. In this he employed to particular effect an oratorical device which was to end every sentence with the word 'but. . .'. Before his opponents could realise that the conjunction actually disguised the end of a sentence, he had marshalled his thoughts and was off again.

Browne, by contrast, is dark, sallow, and quiet, but with

considerable oratorical skills which he would deploy to considerable effect at Labour Party Conferences, his voice sinking to a whisper or rising to a declamation with equal ease. He would frequently sit by himself in a corner of the room in which the PLP meetings were held, head in hands, to all intents and purposes in another world. Then, apropos of what seemed to be nothing in particular, he would unleash a scorching attack on some or all of his colleagues, rounding with particular acerbity on his party leader, and on occasion stalking out of the room before another word could be spoken.

Nobody could possibly emulate the number of guises under which Browne has appeared in Dail and Seanad Eireann, and tracing his political career is a tortuous exercise in an ideological as much as in an institutional sense. Born in Waterford in 1915, his father died when he was seven. A childhood of considerable poverty and deprivation was followed by the most extraordinary good fortune, as a Dublin family befriended him and all but adopted him, enabling him to secure educational advantages which he later was to put to such scintillating effect. After education at a minor English public school and at Trinity College, Dublin, where he qualified as a doctor, he began his long and fitful journey, through various forms of political martyrdom (some of them self-inflicted, his critics would maintain), towards his present position of lonely eminence on the Left, still to some degree an idol of the media, still capable of attracting an audience, especially in Dublin, even in his seventies. His status as a loner is, in a sense, part of his attractiveness to many people. It is tempting, when trying to analyse it, to think of Peadar O'Donnell's answer to the questioner who asked him why he was not a member of a political party: 'I've always been a member of a political party', O'Donnell replied on that occasion, 'even though I could never find any other member of it besides myself. And, even at that, opinion within the party has not always been unanimous.'

So many of the stands Browne took were inconsistent with positions he took later that it is difficult to detect a common thread, but some components can perhaps be disinterred from the rhetoric with which he has mounted his campaigns. One of them is his reaction as a young doctor, who amazingly became both a TD and a minister for the first time on the same day, to the lamentable state of Irish health care which had marked his own family's life for many years. This led him, over a long period of time, into ever more radical policy positions. Another has been his growing conviction that the institutional Catholic Church has been responsible for more of the things that are wrong with Ireland than any other single force. A third is his undying opposition to Fine Gael, especially on health policy matters.

The growing radicalisation—perhaps in itself quite explicable in someone who has spent such a long time in politics, and who was as conditioned by his early environment as anyone else—can be readily evidenced by some of the early positions he took, even if the temper of the times he lived in marked some of his other utterances more conservatively. In 1949, for example, he delivered a speech (undoubtedly written for him by some zealot in the Department of Health, or perhaps extracted as part of some wider negotiations in relation to private hospitals) which contained an extraordinary denial of the need for sex education for young people 'in view of the moral integrity and strong family life which results from the moral and religious teaching so readily and widely available in this country'. Of course, times change. Perhaps if we had all been making speeches more than thirty-five years ago we might have been saying something very similar, but the contrast with his more recent attitudes is certainly striking. Again, during his tussle with the Catholic hierarchy—and with his own party superiors—over the Mother and Child Scheme, he made it clear that his defiance was based on advice he had received to the effect that his proposals were only contrary to Catholic social, and not moral, teaching. The inference was that if Catholic moral teaching had been involved, he might have taken a different position. But again, knowing Noel, he might not. In 1952 he welcomed a Fianna Fail White Paper on health services despite the fact that it contained no fewer than three means tests, and in the same year voted with Fianna Fail, as an independent, to abolish food subsidies on the grounds that 'the alternative government would not give any assurance that if elected they would not do the same thing'. This led, many years later, to a typically bitter exchange when, at the Labour Party Conference in Cork in 1970 which overturned the party's decision not to go into coalition, Browne shouted 'Shame! Shame!' at Brendan Corish, to be met with the retort, 'I never shouted "Shame" when you voted to abolish food subsidies.'

65

After the collapse of the Inter-party government, he resigned from Clann na Poblachta (for which party he had originally been elected) in 1951 and spent some time as an independent before apparently making a first, unsuccessful attempt to join the Labour Party. After this failed, he applied to and was accepted by Fianna Fail, a party of which he said in 1954 when they in turn lost office that he was proud to be a member, and proud to be associated with some of the men who took part in so many tremendously important events in the history of the country. His sojourn in Fianna Fail was not to be a long one, but there is no denying that he had his followers in that party, being elected to the National Executive in 1957. He also had his critics, including Eamon de Valera. On one occasion, Dev shared a winter rural by-election campaign with the young Browne who spoke of Fianna Fail as the party of the poor, the hungry and the dispossessed, as the snowflakes swirled around the platform party, and with the passion that only Browne could muster. Later, on the way back to Dublin in his official car, Dev wondered, half-aloud, to his companion how on earth such a person could ever have been allowed into Fianna Fail.

Eventually refusing a Fianna Fail nomination in 1957, he was expelled from the party after standing as an independent. In 1958 he founded the National Progressive Democrats with Jack McQuillan, for years the only left-wing TD from West of the Shannon. The NPD was in fact briefly attractive to a number of people who saw, as they thought, the makings of a new Clann na Poblachta. They included myself, who was introduced to, and enrolled in, the party as a university student in Dublin by Owen Dudley Edwards, and even issued with a membership card.

Browne's long and elliptical journey towards the Labour Party finally ended in 1963, when he and McQuillan joined together, liquidating the NPD in the progress. It was the start of a twenty-year relationship which was to have more than its share of bitterness, upheaval and rebellion. It took some time, however, before the rebel actually tangled with his party on a point of discipline. At one stage, for example, even though he was prepared to go on record as supporting the demand by Irish homosexuals for a change in the laws which criminalised their adult behaviour, he stopped short of any commitment to bring legislation into the PLP or before the Dail on the grounds that public opinion was not ready for it. In this, indeed, he may well have been expressing a solicitude, not for public opinion as such, but for the tender political susceptibilities of most of his colleagues on the PLP, who would undoubtedly have been struck rigid with horror at the prospect of putting their names to such an initiative. In later years, still in the party but a voluntary exile from its parliamentary wing, he was to exercise a role as *franc-tireur* that made his earlier caution look positively reticent.

His opposition to the Catholic Church, although it undoubtedly had its origins in the Mother and Child controversy, did not achieve its full flowering until quite a few years later. It is basically a hostility to the Church as an institution, and it coexists quite equably in his politics with feelings of admiration for individual Churchmen and women, more particularly those involved in the care of the mentally handicapped. This can be partly traced, too, to the strength of his feelings for his own mentally handicapped brother. The intensity of his feelings about the Church, and about coalition with Fine Gael, in fact indicate a relatively limited socialist agenda, and one confined chiefly—but effectively—to the social sphere. Thus, he has tended not to seek a high profile on the economic issues which other members of the party—people like Halligan, Keating, Cluskey and Higgins— tended to concentrate on, preferring to direct his undoubted firepower towards what he perceives as the major obstacle to social progress in Ireland.

Although the timing may have been coincidental, the full exposition of his thought on this matter, in a famous speech in 1971, added to the ructions that were already going on in the PLP. Now, just as there was a group of TDs who wanted to expel Stevie Coughlan for his utterances in Limerick, Coughlan and his allies wanted to discipline Browne for his attack on the Catholic Church, which they believed would do them untold damage in their constituencies. The controversy was eventually patched up, or at least patched over, and the two warring factions were to remain in their respective corners, glowering at each other, for another two years.

The attractiveness of Browne's position for a certain kind of Irish voter can perhaps be partly explained by his anti-clericalism, which finds a readily understandable echo in a country in which one Church has been dominant for so long. Sometimes, indeed, it can look to an outside observer as if anti-clericalism, in Ireland, is synonymous with socialism, despite the fact that there is no necessary or umbilical connection. In other words, socialists can be—indeed often are, in Ireland—anti-clerical, but anti-clericals are not necessarily socialists. In much the same way, his opposition to coalition—which it is more accurate to say is an opposition to Fine Gael—is a stance which is not necessarily socialist, and which therefore will ensure a wider following outside the party. 'Fine Gael', he remarked as long ago as January 1954, 'must be pursued, harried and attacked continuously, and rooted out of public life when possible'. One irony is that many of the people who look up to him as an instinctive opponent of coalition do not know, or have forgotten, that he has never made opposition to socialism a principle. Indeed, at one conference which re-affirmed the electoral strategy Browne, winding up the debate for the anti-coalition side, dismayed his followers more than a little when he prefaced his speech by saying that coalition for him was not a matter of principle one way or the other.

He declined to seek a nomination for the Dail in 1973, and ran instead on the Dublin University constituency for the Seanad, where he was comfortably elected by probably the least working-class electorate in Ireland, if not in the world. His election agent in this contest was David Thornley, who had just lost his own Cabra seat, and whom I met in Leinster House just before the Seanad nomination papers went in. 'I'm just about to do one of the most extraordinary things I've ever done', David exclaimed excitedly. His on-off relationship with Browne, however—he had worked for Noel when Noel stood as an independent as far back as 1957—was to be ruptured again before the end. During his four years in the Seanad, Browne remained a member of the party, but did not apply for membership of the PLP, which left him in what was, to other members of the party, an enviable position: free to criticise, to oppose and even to denounce, without having to shoulder the often burdensome weight of collective responsibility. Conscious of the possibility of Browne being selected for a Dail constituency by a Labour constituency organisation at the following election, and equally conscious that there was nothing in the rule book to prevent this, the AC promptly changed the rules to ensure that he would not be eligible. The party organisation—and many longtime Browne supporters—in Dublin North-East

(Mr Haughey's constituency) decided to defy the AC, and went ahead and selected him as a candidate regardless. Again he was comfortably re-elected, this time to the Dail.

The apprehension with which his former colleagues in the PLP viewed his return can be imagined, all the more so when they saw that the first twenty or so motions on the Dail order paper for private members' time had been put down by Browne before either the Labour or Fine Gael whips had had time to sort out their priorities. Worse again, Browne's shopping list included every subject, from divorce through contraception to ending clerical control of education, designed to send a frisson through every Right-minded conservative, in no matter what party. According to Standing Orders, he could have insisted on a debate on each and every one of them in turn, but with that failure to finish a brilliant move off effectively which has marked much of his career in politics, he was not even present in the chamber at the appropriate moment to move his resolutions, and the whips, with a collective sigh of relief, gratefully resumed control of the business of the house.

His brief period of membership of the Socialist Labour Party—despite the fact that he was the only member of the party in the Dail he refused, in a typical display of idiosyncrasy, to consider himself the party's parliamentary spokesman—ended when the party began to tear itself to shreds over the Northern Ireland issue. Since then he has effectively retired to Connemara to write, and not even efforts made in person by two successive Labour leaders have managed to tempt him back. The first was in January 1982, when Browne rejected an open invitation by the then Labour leader, Michael O'Leary, to stand as a party candidate. In April of the same year he was asked to stand in the Dublin West by-election created by Dick Burke's second departure to Brussels, but again refused, no doubt less because he lacked the appetite for a contest than because he had the seasoned campaigner's instinct for the likely outcome. After O'Leary's departure he was asked to run for Dublin North-Central, but responded, 'I would do everything I could to help Dick Spring, but he has to make it clear that the Labour Party is being run by him and not by the rump who have brought it to where it is today. If that rump is still in control, I'm not interested.'

Even in his refusal, in effect, he paid unconscious homage to his (and perhaps other people's) idea of the Labour Party as a collection of dedicated socialists whose every political wish has been frustrated by the activities of a 'rump'. The image, too, of Dick Spring as a benign socialist dictator within the party—as if the party should and could be 'run' by any individual, no matter how powerful—betrays a strongly individualist streak. The nature of the Labour Party, as he might have been expected to recognise after three decades, is somewhat more complex, and the Coughlans and the other members of the Munster Mafia, as they were called, against whom he pitted himself with at least as much ferocity as he opposed Fianna Fail and Fine Gael, were in reality neither a rump nor a majority, but an historical carryover that simply would not evaporate, and to some degree remains in existence today.

Browne's *hubris*, if that is the right word for it, has always been a tendency to spoil a splendid argument or piece of oratory with a personalised attack, usually in his peroration. The classic example of this was during the Galway Conference of 1974, when he embarked on a sustained critique of coalition and Labour's role in it that had the delegates almost eating out of his hand—and then blew it with a savage attack directed personally at Brendan Corish, then Tanaiste as well as party leader, who was sitting on the platform. The party in government may have been guilty of many or even all of the charges he levelled at it, but not even the bitterest critic of coalition elsewhere in the hall would stand for this tactic, and Browne's support melted away in moments.

The choice of individuals to represent the rebels on the Left and Right of the party is always to some degree arguable, but Browne and Coughlan represent these extremes with some clarity. This is not to say that there were not others, even if some of them were part-time rebels, or rebels on one issue only. The main difference between the two groups was that those on the Right were, by and large, considerably less vulnerable electorally than those on the Left, and could ignore party policy as well as party discipline when it suited them. This was particularly true of the Right after 1969, when the advent of the 'intellectuals' caused many of the rural deputies to give a fair imitation of political hermit crabs. It was widely rumoured within the party during the seventies, for example, that the railway stations at both Tralee and Cork possessed the largest collection in Ireland of unused—

because uncollected—Labour Party general election posters. Neither Dan Spring nor Michael Pat Murphy were too anxious to be publicly identified with such alien growths. In 1969, too, the AC, in a flush of enthusiasm which was to result in the crash of lost deposits in constituencies all over the country, decreed that all sitting deputies should take a running mate in the campaign. It fell to Brendan Halligan to inform Dan Spring that, should he fail to do so, he would be expelled from the party. After the election—in which he had totally ignored the ruling—Spring met Halligan again. 'Are you going to expel me?' he enquired.

Party discipline aside, of course, it is always the so-called 'moral' issues which have given the right-wing members of the party in the Dail most cause for rebellion. The contraception debate in 1985 provided a classic example of this when two deputies—Frank Prendergast of Limerick and Sean Treacy of Tipperary—defied, and lost, the party whip. The strangest thing of all about this particular episode, given that a small parliamentary party like Labour will always go to considerable lengths to avoid reducing its Dail strength for any longer than is absolutely necessary, was not that the two deputies lost the whip, but that only one of them— Prendergast—returned to the fold. There was undoubtedly a personal as well as a political element in the conflict between the Tipperary deputy and the new young leader of the party. It may even have gained in bitterness because of the leader's decision not to allocate any governmental responsibilities to the former Ceann Comhairle. Whatever it was, it was enough to prevent the breach healing over. The lack of tears at Treacy's departure was, perhaps, an indication of the degree to which the party was changing, even though it was still, in the eyes of many of its supporters, not changing quickly enough.

Of the other rebels on the Left, few stand out, with the possible exception of Michael Mullen, and of course David Thornley, although placing David on the Left of the party was always a somewhat hazardous exercise. He fulfilled the role of left-wing rebel in only one major respect: his opposition to the 1973–77 Coalition's security legislation. This, in retrospect, can be seen to have had more to do with his background as the child of passionately Republican parents than with left-wing ideology *per se*. As early as 1971 he was on record as saying, in relation to the North, that the use of force could not be ruled out in all circumstances. His highly emotional nature and a recurring health problem led him to make many statements from which he later had to climb down: being David, the climb-downs were always executed with the maximum of wit, whatever the ultimate cost to his political credibility. In June 1972, speaking at a Mansion House meeting on the Prisons Bill of that year, he described his own party as 'temporarily berserk': not long after that, his spokesmanship was downgraded from Education to Posts and Telegraphs, and in September of the same year he ceased to be chairman of the important Administrative Sub-Committee of the AC. With Noel Browne, he at first declined to sign the fourteen-point plan on which the incoming Coalition fought the 1973 election. Unlike Browne, he later signed.

His passionately-held Catholicism (he used to sing in the Westland Row choir) did not prevent him from espousing party policy wholeheartedly in a number of areas, not least in relation to contraception. Appointed as a member of the European Parliament in Strasbourg (partly to get him out of the way, it was suggested, as Strasbourg parliamentarians got an automatic 'pair' in most Leinster House votes), he was infuriated when the famous Contraception Bill, for which he had been brought back from Strasbourg to vote, was defeated after the Taoiseach, Liam Cosgrave, and other Fine Gael TDs had voted with Fianna Fail against the measure. Writing to the government chief whip later to express his indignation, Thornley noted:

> I shall have, in future, to consult my conscience, my wife, my confessor and the cat, in that order, before I decide whether to turn up or not. I shall not, of course, consult my colleagues, since that seems to be out of fashion. Kindest good wishes to both of you (Kelly and Barry Desmond, the Labour whip) in the difficult mission to which the Lord has assigned you. I trust that your consciences will always be 'informed'. Jesus help us. David.

Copies of the full text of the letter were obtained and eagerly distributed by members of the Fianna Fail party in Leinster House the day after it had been written!

Nor was his nationalism of the Catholic variety. He took particular exception to clerical intervention in human sexuality, especially when it was combined with political irredentism. This evoked a famous 1972 letter to *The Irish Times*:

Sir,—If I have to open my *Irish Times* once more to imbibe the pontifications of the celibate Father Denis Faul on the mysterious workings of the male and female sexual organs, I confess I shall bring up my breakfast over page 11 of your admirable newspaper—a serious, if not unnatural, use of bacon and newsprint (cf. Aquinas). This is the same Fr Faul who bemoans (quite rightly) British rule in Northern Ireland. So the Northern Liberal is to embrace (chastely) the South provided that he places his or her genitalia under the broad supervision of the Dungannon Academy. Have we all lost our sense of humour? If Faul or Faulkner, give me Faulkner: at least our separated brethren can sneak North to purchase furtively and smuggle back discreetly what in their ignorance they regard to be their natural right. It is the Fauls who cause the Paisleys.

In 1975, he was explaining his decision to vote for the Criminal Justice Bill. 'I detest it. Loathe it. I hope it will be made unconstitutional . . . but that does not make me a man of violence. That just makes me a realist. There is nothing they (his critics) would like better than that I should ride off into the sunset on a white horse—like John Wayne, only slightly shorter and slightly fatter.'

Like Noel Browne, he had been a member of the National Progressive Democrats (he left after a year) but his close feelings of admiration for Browne later soured, and he was to strike up an extraordinary relationship with deputies like Stevie Coughlan and Dan Spring, whom he seemed to see as the essential grass roots of the Labour Party. He saw their power base as essential, he once said, to thwart the efforts of Noel Browne and others on the doctrinaire Left who might take the party on a 'pilgrimage to frustration'. He defended Coughlan at the 1972 Conference, but such a gesture was not reciprocated when, as noted earlier, the whip was withdrawn from him: only Dan Spring, of the rural deputies, voted against removal of the whip (with John O'Connell and Michael D. Higgins).

After a brief period as member of the SLP, he was re-admitted to the PLP in February 1977, and his final election campaign was a disaster: in the constituency in which, eight years previously, he had polled two thousand votes over the quota, he was to lose his deposit. After that election he recalled, in an interview, what his wife Petria had said to him when he told her of his original decision to join the Labour Party, 'It was inevitable. It will kill you'. On 16 June, a year later, he was admitted to intensive care, and three days later he was dead.

His wayward Republicanism mirrored—although much more colourfully and ultimately more tragically—that of John O'Connell, another party rebel who was ultimately to join Fianna Fail, in what was perhaps one of the most spectacular reversals of a personally-held position ever witnessed in the party. O'Connell, although personally gregarious, always operated as a loner, not least within the PLP. His combination of fierce competitiveness and ruthlessness made him as awkward a colleague as an opponent, as a number of his running-mates in Ballyfermot found out to their cost. But it was on the question of the North that his capacity for stirring things up was seen at its best. He had—or claimed to have—a permanent hot-line to the Provisional IRA. On one occasion at a PLP meeting he offered to ring them up from a phone in the corner of the room. His actions in arranging a secret meeting in Dublin between Harold Wilson and the Provisional leadership, without the knowledge of his own party leader, almost led to his expulsion.

A medical doctor, and certainly the wealthiest member of the PLP (his *Irish Medical Times*, a hugely successful medical publication, was later sold to a British publishing company, and he also edited *MIMS*, the Irish drug directory) he almost certainly felt keenly the fact that he had never been offered even a junior ministerial position, when such was on offer. He jumped at the chance to run for the European Parliament, and was elected after a campaign which was a peculiarly brilliant combination of American-style razzmatazz and native Irish parish pumpery. It was only after he had been elected that he began to explore the consequences of what had happened and—for he abhorred flying—blanched at the prospect of the amount of travel involved. He failed to make any mark at all in Europe, and his subsequent action in declining to resign from Strasbourg for some time after he had been nominated as Ceann Comhairle must have done his reputation little good among many of the people who had voted for him.

The possibility is, of course, that they would have voted for him for other reasons. His attention to the minutiae of political activity in his constituency was legendary, as was his control over his own constituency organisation. When the Fianna Fail TD Noel Lemass died, necessitating a by-election in Ballyfermot, it was acknowledged ruefully by O'Connell's colleagues that they would have little say in choosing the Labour candidate. It was therefore with something approaching apoplexy that they heard him suggest, at one meeting of the PLP, that Noel Browne might be the candidate (Browne was at this time a senator, although without the party whip, and a considerable thorn in the party's flesh). That particular proposal came to nothing, and it was not even certain whether O'Connell himself had actually supported it personally. The sequel was even more astonishing, when the selection convention chose, on O'Connell's proposal, the then general secretary of the party, Brendan Halligan. Halligan, astounded, heard the news for the first time on his car radio. He was reluctant to accept, but his instincts were overruled by his loyalty to Brendan Corish, who suggested to him that a refusal would look like a vote of no confidence in the Coalition government which was then in office.

Halligan won the by-election, but it was the beginning of the end of his parliamentary career. O'Connell gave a public undertaking that Halligan would remain in the constituency which everyone, not least O'Connell, knew could not and would not be honoured. In fact, O'Connell told Halligan later that the reason why he had chosen him as the candidate was because he (Halligan) was an intelligent man who would realise that there was not room for both of them in the constituency. A less percipient by-election winner, O'Connell suggested, might have made his (O'Connell's) life a misery in the belief that the two seats could both be retained at the next electoral outing.

When O'Connell finally left the party it was hardly with many regrets on either side. When he joined Fianna Fail, however, during that party's extraordinary and opportunistic opposition to Barry Desmond's Family Planning Bill in 1985, there were not a few who remembered his own statement of conscience just over a decade earlier, 'We are hypocrites if we start talking about denial of rights in Northern Ireland when we refuse to grant the right of people here to practise contraception . . . I do not think we should discriminate between single and married people.'

Apart from individual rebels, there are of course a number of rebel groups, if rebel is not too picturesque a word to use in all such cases. A loose association of people known as 'Labour Left', includes AC members such as Councillor Frank Buckley, Councillor Emmett Stagg, Ita Kavanagh, Joe O'Callaghan, Angie O'Leary and Michael O'Reilly. It does not seem to have the broad base of its predecessor of the seventies, the Liaison of the Left, but it is more professional, and its publication *Labour Left*, which got off the ground when Brendan Halligan was a member of the European Parliament, is a glossier, more confident production than anything which the party headquarters has so far managed to produce in the same line. Its other main difference from the Liaison grouping is the apparent welcome it received for a time at Head Office, although this welcome was eventually withdrawn. As a group, it probably is of less significance, in terms of Labour's overall structure of quarrelsome socialism, than the so-called 'Militant Tendency'.

The Militant organisation, or the Mafia Tendency as it is sometimes called, exemplifies a current of thought which has existed since Trotsky's day, and which claims him as a guru (as indeed do other Left groups opposed to the Militants—just to make matters more confusing). In some countries, where it exists at all, it takes the form of a separate political entity. In Ireland and England, however, it has chosen to attach itself to the Labour Party in each country, within which it maintains a fundamentally parasitic existence. In doing so it perpetuates the technique advocated by Trotsky himself, when he proposed 'entryism'—a technique involving the penetration of the French socialist organisations by his supporters. Its operations in Britain, where it has existed since 1950, are better documented than in Ireland, but there has been cooperation between the British and Irish parties on information about it. Shirley Williams—a Labour MP at the time—described its adherents as 'termites burrowing their way towards the heart of the party', and certainly it was evident that by 1978 at least ten per cent of delegates from the constituencies to the British Labour Party's annual conference were members of this particular tendency. Its objectives may, at least on paper, overlap those of the parent organisation at certain points, but are for the most part irrelevant to the kind of political choices being offered to, and made by, the electorate as a whole. The organisation's chief strategy, in effect, is to advance what are known as 'transitional demands'—demands on non-revolutionary socialists which they know cannot be accepted, and are designed to discredit democratic socialism and win converts for insurrectionary politics. Its transitional demands—at least as far as 1985 went— were expressed by Angie O'Leary, one of Labour Youth's representatives on the AC, with a familiarly deceptive clairty, 'Break Coalition Now! For a national minimum wage of £120 a week! For the nationalisation of the banks and major industry! For a socialist plan of production to end poverty and the jobs crisis!'

It is given to somewhat jaded rhetoric. 'This government' wrote Dermot Connolly, a contributor to their Irish newspaper in May 1985, 'and the right-wing Labour leaders who prop it up, must be propelled from office. The powerful trade union movement, with over 500,000 members, must be mobilised to smash this government and bring back the Labour Party into the hands of the working class.'

The organisation has failed, despite more than thirty years of political activity in these islands, to secure an answering response from the trade union movement it idolises. This may have something to do with the editorial opinion expressed in the same issue of the paper that trade union officials should be subject to recall by the rank and file, and should not be paid more than the average wage of those they represent. And their faith in the Irish trade union movement is put in a somewhat peculiar light by their decision to have their monthly newspaper, *Militant*, printed in England.

Characterised by a rather narrow dogmatism (veering at times into fanaticism), the endless repetition of slogans masquerading as policies, and a certain Puritan humourlessness, the Militants represent every right-winger's view of the lunatic Left, a kind of political Moonie sect. Superficially, their slogans seem simple and indeed have the attractiveness of all simplistic solutions to complex problems. Embellished with much martial rhetoric drawn, it seems, from the now quaintly inflammatory pamphlets that went out of fashion thirty years ago or more, their slogans call for smashing the capitalist system, forcing the two capitalist parties, Fianna Fail and Fine Gael, into alignment with each other (if only it were that easy), and a workers' mass movement dominated by the trade unions. On one occasion their revolutionary zeal deserted them in dramatic circumstances. This was when, during one of Labour Youth's annual conferences in Liberty Hall, the building was besieged by a large and angry crowd of Sinn Fein supporters (this was during the hunger strikes in the Maze). The many Militant supporters within the building found the opportunity to address such a large and potentially revolutionary assembly of the working class distinctly resistible.

They are characterised, not only by their ideology, but by a peculiar manner of addressing public meetings, the words delivered in a monotone accompanied by a robot-like chopping motion of the right hand. This appears to have been borrowed in part from the style of Ted Grant, the English leader of the tendency. It was developed even further by John Throne, the original guru of the tendency in the Irish Labour Party, and is to some degree continued, although in a weakened form, by the present arbiter of the movement, Joe Higgins, an elected member of the AC. Higgins, who comes from a farming background in West Kerry, is also a fluent Irish speaker. His accent, like that of other Militants, betrays at times curious Liverpudlian overtones which can also be traced back to Grant's style. He is an able organiser, and gave up a teaching job to work full-time for his organisation, as do an unspecified number of other supporters of the group—some of them unemployed, others probably remunerated on a cooperative basis by their income from donations and subscriptions.

They exact financial dues from each other with all the enthusiasm of a primitive monastic community, and collect energetically to support their own distinct organisation and newspaper. Their success on these fronts can be seen from the fact that they employ a number of people in their Abbey Street office and that their paper has stayed afloat (thanks to a degree of self-subsidisation) where attempts to start a Labour Party newspaper have ignominiously failed. Irish Militancy's neo-syndicalist flag-waving can be a great source of attractiveness to some young people in that it provides, within a Labour Party which cannot really be relied upon to abstain from the fleshpots of government, a focus of permanent opposition—whether to the government, the system, or the party leadership is ultimately, in a sense, immaterial.

The leadership of Labour Youth is now completely controlled

by this sub-group within the party—a fact which has given the party hierarchy some cause for concern for a number of years. When Brendan Halligan was general secretary, he got a considerable quantity of documentation from Britain about Militant activities there. Frank Cluskey, when leader, suggested at an AC meeting before the 1981 election that it might be appropriate to carry out an investigation into the organisation. After the election, he was no longer leader, and so much turbulence attended Michael O'Leary's leadership that the Militant question rarely got on to the agenda.

Dick Spring clearly thought, at one stage, that this problem needed to be tackled, and proposed an investigation of the organisation to see whether or not it infringed the section of the party constitution which lays down that a member of the party shall not be 'a member of any other political party or of an organisation ancillary thereto' (3.1). A change of tactics then ensued, and the proposed investigation was aborted. It is difficult to see, with hindsight, how Militant and its supporters could construe such a decision other than as a sign of weakness or indecision. A flanking movement was inaugurated at the 1985 Conference when an AC motion urged delegates to give party branches in third level educational institutions enhanced status within Labour Youth, not least because third level educational institutions have proved poor recruiting grounds for Militant. The degree of elitism inherent in the motion was, however, skilfully attacked by Militant speakers, and it was defeated.

The advisability or non-advisability of expelling Militant members from the party is keenly debated within the party hierarchy. The party chairman, Michael D. Higgins, once featured as a donor in the list of supporters published regularly in their newspaper, and there is a strong Militant presence within his Galway West constituency. Although not Militant himself he is, however, like many other Left members of the party, opposed to expulsions almost on principle, and the question, if not resolved rapidly, may soon become somewhat academic, if the tendency grows to the extent that expelling its members simply becomes a political impossibility. This will happen if Left and liberal members of the party, who may have had little experience of the interminable infighting that accompanies any Militant attempt to take over any section of the party, and who are temperamentally or even politically opposed to expulsions, rally to their defence. The situation has achieved a level of public visibility that is in itself new: Stephen Collins, an *Irish Press* political reporter, noted with a mixture of amusement and puzzlement at the 1985 Conference in Cork that 'Spot the Militant is a game played by long suffering Labour delegates who have to listen to a stream of earnest young men and women preaching about the evils of capitalism and the mortal sin of coalition.'

The truth probably is that Militant could not exist without the Labour Party to act as a life-support system. Internal bulletins of the organisation make no pretence that Militant is nothing more than a newspaper with supporters, but refer to it straightforwardly as an 'organisation' with recruitment drives, membership, organisers and national conferences. Restricted to the senior members of the party's hierarchy, they are also designed to make the detection of individuals difficult by mentioning names only when unavoidable, and by restricting usage of the phrase 'Revolutionary Socialist League' to members of its inner sanctum.

It is difficult to escape the impression that the Irish Labour Party is waiting for the Labour Party in Britain to take more definite steps in relation to expelling the vast bulk of Militant members (some have already been expelled) before taking an initiative on this side of the Irish Sea. The problem raised by this tactic, however, is that Militant obviously poses a much greater threat to a small organisation like the Irish Labour Party than it does to its much larger counterpart in Britain. It is not even necessary to identify the threat too specifically. Even if Militant does no more than soak up some of the energies that should be used to expand Labour's organisation and win Dail seats, even if it never extends its tentacles to any serious degree beyond Labour Youth, it will continue to be numbered among the many forces which help to keep Labour on the margins of Irish political life, and its well-meaning defenders will be making the mistake of confusing sentiment with professionalism. Either way, the Militants give all the other rebels a bad name.

4

Country Cousins

IN THE second half of the 1960s, a coup took place in the Labour Party—but it was a coup which was only partly successful. Many supporters of the old regime retreated into the hinterland and kept their powder dry, waiting for an opportunity to strike back. In 1970 they got that chance, and they took it with both hands.

This, no doubt slightly over-simplified, analysis offers us the best perspective for looking at both the vexed question of coalition and the related question of whether there are not one but several Labour parties in existence, conveniently grouped under the same banner.

The Labour Party up to 1965 or thereabouts in fact exhibited many of the tendencies of a political organisation which had become very set in its ways. Jimmy Tully, as party chairman on a number of occasions, had set his own very individual stamp on the character of the party: so had Molly Davidson as general secretary. The party could not hold a candle to its competitors in organisational, financial or professional terms. The party was not, in fact, organised at all in the accepted sense of the word, in that it had no central register of membership, no income worth speaking of, and a tiny staff which was subvented partly by the device of ensuring the election of the general secretary to the Seanad.

In 1966 Brendan Halligan became political advisor to the party leader, Brendan Corish. The position had been advertised, and there was a short list of some thirty people (the Labour Party tendency to solve its problems by adding to them being as evident then as now) which included, among other distinguished applicants, Michael Farrell, later of the People's Democracy and now a freelance journalist. Whether it had been the explicit intention of those who proposed this innovation at Head Office or not, Halligan became general secretary the following year when Molly Davidson resigned. As when Seamus Scally succeeded him more than a decade later, the post was not actually advertised, and the heir-apparent simply moved one step up the hierarchy at the bidding of the AC.

Nor was this the only change. A Commission was set up under the chairmanship, initially, of Proinsias MacAonghusa, and whose members included both Niall Greene (chairman of the latest) party commission on electoral strategy) and Michael O'Leary. This Commission made a number of hard-headed recommendations about the structures and finances which were accepted by conference and put into effect: the party had begun to function as a political machine for what was probably the first time. Nor was the input confined to the organisational level. At the political level, new deputies like O'Leary, Cluskey and Desmond were busy upping the ideological *ante*. Behind them, in every positive sense of the word, were people like Greene and Donal Nevin, now general secretary of the Irish Congress of Trade Unions, who was an active organiser and occasional director of elections in the Dublin area.

When Brendan Corish, at the 1967 Party Conference, launched his policy initiative, calling on the party to develop socialist policies more in keeping with the times than the somewhat unadorned anti-coalition stance which had been its trademark up to then, people like these were only too ready to take advantage of it. Barry Desmond in particular was a tireless committee worker, and as chairman of the party for a time had the unique opportunity, not only to make an input into policy formulation, but (as some of his critics within the party dourly noted) to anticipate it in public with a series of well-timed speeches advocating new policies for Labour which were delivered just as one or other of the various sub-committees finished their drafting of the policy in question.

The two policy conferences of 1968 and 1969 marked the high point of the new regime's control of the party—or, to be more precise, of its ideological stance. As later events were to show, control of the party as a whole was much more problematic. The old guard appeared to have melted away. At the 1969 Conference only Jimmy Tully, no longer party chairman but sitting with his own constituency delegates at the back of the hall, intervened to criticise the new policy departures (as late as 1972 he was arguing trenchantly against the nationalisation of the country's mineral resources).

But people who have formed the backbone of a political party (however calcified) for several decades simply do not disappear: and the result of the 1969 election was to show that, when finally roused, they were still a force to be reckoned with. With the benefit of hindsight, it is difficult to avoid the impression that the initial reaction of TDs like Tom Kyne, Dan Spring, Sean Treacy, Stevie Coughlan, John Ryan and Michael Pat Murphy—the 'rednecks' of the party, as Michael D. Higgins was to describe them (although not by name) pungently in a 1985 interview—was that all this policy-making was a harmless enough activity which would not have any serious electoral effect and, moreover, kept some of these young radicals from attempting anything more dangerous. Nor was their anti-coalitionism the bright and shiny suit of armour it represented for some of the newer TDs in the party, like Michael O'Leary: it was more like a comfortable set of old clothes. They did not make the connection then—if they ever thought about it—between the new-fangled policies and their prospects of entering into government, in that the internal logic of the new policies was to make coalition a much less likely option than it had been hitherto.

Politicians like Jack Lynch were more perspicacious, and lost no opportunity, before and during the 1969 general election campaign, of labelling the Labour Party as a hotbed of extremist subversives. Conor Cruise O'Brien, often given to pulling the pin out of an electoral hand-grenade and then forgetting to throw it away, became part of this mythology in record time with two relatively off-the-cuff remarks, one advocating the closure of our embassy in Portugal (and the opening of one in Cuba) and the other suggesting that it was sectarian to broadcast the Angelus on RTE television. The 1969 election was known by some journalists as the 'convent election' from Lynch's habit of making well-publicised visits to as many religious institutions as possible to underwrite his party's perception that Labour represented a real political threat. Despite the recent Vatican Council, it was still assumed, in those days, that all the residents of such institutions voted obediently in the manner indicated by their religious superiors. And, if Lynch's campaign was more of a nudge and a wink, some of his ministers were more direct: the Minister for Justice, Michael Moran, described Corish as someone in thrall to 'the modern Marxist elite' and Sean MacEntee stated that Labour stood for Lenin, Stalin, and 'the red flames of burning homesteads in Meath'. Not a far cry, perhaps, from the election of two decades earlier in which Fianna Fail had predicted that if they were defeated, the next Minister for Education would be James Larkin, who had been educated in the 'Lenin Academy' in Moscow.

Even before the election campaign had started, there were premonitions at Head Office, and the officially-published 'Notes for Canvassers' tackled the problem with some trenchancy. Responding to the blunt query, 'Are you going to nationalise everything?' the eager Labour canvasser was left in no doubt as to the official line.

'That word is not used even once in any of our policy documents. It's a Fianna Fail smear which says we're going to nationalise industries, the land, shops, the lot in fact. These are lies. Bad ones. We will, in fact, bring some industries under public control where public welfare demands. And we will develop our own resources by state industries instead of leaving it to foreign speculators as in the case of our mining deposits.'

Plainly a poor job was done on the doorsteps in those areas in which the charge could be expected to be most frequently made, for if the results of the 1969 election are examined in some detail it will be seen that whereas they represented a set-back for the party nationally in terms of seats won (the overall total going down by four), they represented a near-disaster in Munster, the area which, atypically, had provided the most solid core of Labour support at the polls for many of the preceding elections. In the previous (1965) general election, Labour in Munster had polled its highest percentage of the vote ever (18.5 per cent) and had won ten seats—including, it should be admitted, the then out-going Ceann Comhairle, Paddy Hogan from Clare, whose Labour seat was to disappear into the Atlantic mists, never to reappear, once he resigned. In 1969, while the overall Labour vote in the country as a whole rose to its highest ever level, and the Labour vote in Dublin rose by an even greater percentage, the decline in Munster had already set in, and Munster's Dail representation was in fact more than halved, from ten to only four seats. Not only that, but the party in Munster had run twice the normal number of candidates (up to twenty-five from a regular figure of between eleven and thirteen), and the clatter of lost deposits formed a sort of *obbligato* to the keening of the displaced deputies.

It is natural for people who have been booted in the electoral midriff so savagely to look around for someone or something to blame, and the 'Munster Mafia', as they are generally known, were not slow to pick their target. In a personal sense it was Brendan Corish himself, who had overseen, and apparently even encouraged, the shift to a socialist rhetoric and to socialist policies, who evoked this ire, especially from a former TD from Cork North-East, Paddy McAuliffe, who later left the party and, standing as an independent, helped to make it unlikely that a Labour candidate would be elected again in that constituency for a very long time. But TDs like Tom Kyne in Waterford had also lost out, as had Eileen Desmond, who had won a spectacular by-election in mid-Cork. And by the time the first post-mortem was held—the party conference was held in private in Liberty Hall—there was a smell of sulphur in the air. At that conference, in fact, a composite resolution which would have committed the party to abandon not only its anti-coalition strategy but also the policies on which it had expended so much energy over the previous five years, was only narrowly deflected by the platform: when the break with anti-coalitionism came at the special conference towards the end of that year, the policy area, at least, remained intact.

It would be unrealistic to put such a traumatic reversal of strategy down solely to the strength and influence of the Munster Mafia: plainly other factors were at work, such as the growing apprehension (and not only within Labour) that Fianna Fail were intent on creating a one-party state in all but name, and the fear of an imminent election for which Labour would be singularly unprepared. But the two latter factors on their own are not sufficient to explain such a diametric shift of attitude, and one possible conclusion, at least, is that those rural deputies and their organisations which had gone along with the new policies for as long as these did not seem to threaten them in any way had now decided that enough was enough. The original series of policy decision, in other words, had been decisions by default: the support they had got from the rural deputies had always been conditional (although this had never been stated) and was now being dramatically withdrawn.

The stage was now set for a re-assertion, by the more traditional groupings within the party, of the degree of control over the organisation which they had hitherto enjoyed. Once bitten, twice shy, and the alternation of coalition with Fianna Fail governments in the fifteen years since that particular 1970 Conference, with the concomitant need to deliver a majority of the votes at the party's now frequent coalition conferences behind the pro-coalition policy of the leadership, has ensured that the mechanism of control has, by and large, remained well-oiled and in good working order.

In this development the Labour Party has tended to mirror developments in Irish politics as a whole. Whereas one school of thought—of which Desmond Fennell, the writer, is a prominent example—tends to argue that Dublin dominates the rest of the country in a thoroughly unequal relationship—there is another analysis which argues that the reverse, in fact, has happened. This point of view argues that the urbanisation of the Dublin region has been so rapid, and has been the product of migration from other parts of Ireland rather than organic in nature, that what has happened in Irish politics has been the domination of the centre by the periphery. This is true to a certain extent even of the politics of the capital. One study by UCD political scientist Tom Garvin has shown that a very high proportion of political activists in one Dublin constituency were in fact only one or two generations removed from their rural roots, and had effectively imported rural politics (with its stress on personal service, its absence of concern for policies as such, and its fondness for patronage in all its shapes and forms) into a twentieth-century city. In the case of the Labour Party, the fact that the greater number of TDs come from outside the Dublin region undoubtedly gives them an edge. So does the fact that the party organisation has, at their insistence, been continuously weighted in their favour.

An interesting, and possibly unique, feature of Labour Party organisation is that there are two types of branches, 'rural' branches and 'urban' branches. The terminology is that of the Constitution itself, and dates from 1980. Up to that time, the Constitution set no formal minimum size for a party branch, and there were some fears that this lacuna encouraged the creation of what were, fairly accurately, known as 'paper branches'—branches whose main function was not to campaign for the party at election time, but to secure the power-base within the party of some local baron or baroness. Even today, it is not unknown for branches to spring up in certain constituencies in response, not to the electoral needs of a given situation, but in response to the creation of other party branches, in a different part of the constituency, by a party colleague/rival. Psephologists within the party claim to discover just such a pattern in the Kildare constituency, for example, where the imminent retirement of the sitting TD, Joe Bermingham, created a major power struggle between two aspirants for his seat—Senator Timmy Conway, (before his departure to join the PDs), and Councillor Emmett Stagg. United in their determination to win the Labour seat, the two men were divided by their attitude on coalition, Stagg opposing it. Knowing that it was only a matter of time before a selection convention was held, both redoubled their efforts to create new branches, with the result that when the roll was finally called in December 1985, there were some fifty branches in the field, divided almost equally between the two contenders. In the event, Conway proved to have been the more successful, in that he not only defeated Stagg by 113 to 95 (each branch at a selection conference has a maximum of four delegates, regardless of size) but, as part of a winner-take-all philosophy, secured the rejection by a roughly similar margin of a recommendation from the AC's organisation committee that, effectively, Stagg should be added to the party ticket. In such circumstances, the location and membership of a new branch will immediately indicate to those in the know exactly which of the two politicians it is likely to support, and the formation of one branch is rapidly matched by the formation of another, like moves in a game of chess. In the case of Kildare, the competition became so intense that the AC actually imposed a moratorium on the creation of new branches.

The received wisdom is that 'paper' branches tend to proliferate in the rural areas, whereas the urban constituencies are hives of independently minded, ideologically committed political activists. Like all generalisations, this is more than a trifle over-simplified. Some rural constituencies—one thinks of Dan Spring's Kerry North, or Michael Pat Murphy's Cork South-West—were undoubtedly organised as personal baronies. On the other hand, urban constituencies could, on occasion, display identical characteristics. There were only six branches in the whole of Dublin for many years, for instance, and only one in Dun Laoghaire, before the period of growth in the sixties. And nobody who participated in the by-election campaign which elected Brendan Halligan in Ballyfermot in 1976 could be under any illusion about that. John O'Connell's constituency machine at that period in his political history was precisely that—a machine. O'Connell himself, Napoleonic in gesture as in stature, directed it with verve and a sense of total control, puffs of smoke marking the hectic departure of his subordinates to all corners of his kingdom at his command. It was rumoured darkly that many of these cohorts, few of whom were ever seen on orthodox party occasions, were, horror of horrors, actually paid by the good doctor. This uncouth lapse into professionalism was then, and would still be, deplored by many Labour Party members who would see it as violating some obscure but unspoken principle, however much they might envy its undoubted effectiveness.

All the talk of differences between 'rural' and 'urban' constituencies tends to miss one important point: that even in the so-called 'rural' constituencies the bulk of the Labour vote probably comes from the towns, and is therefore more properly an urban rather than a rural vote. It is an irony nonetheless that much of the takeover of the party's ideology in the late 1960s was fuelled from outside Dublin, not from inside. Halligan, it is true, is a Dubliner. But both O'Leary and Desmond come from Cork, and Donal Nevin from Limerick. Undoubtedly people like these found the political climate of the capital more congenial. As late as 1977, this trend was still in evidence. Shortly after that election, when I met Jack Lynch in one of the Leinster House corridors, I noted that three of the remaining five Labour TDs in Dublin had Cork origins: O'Leary, Desmond and myself (although born in Tralee, my father was a Corkman). Lynch took a reflective puff on his pipe and remarked mildly, 'You should all be ashamed of yourselves.'

The more conservative party members these had left behind them in the provinces were never without power or influence, no matter what official line had been decided by the party.

This power and influence could, on occasion, be exerted in the crudest possible way—and for all one knows, still is. A classic, if minor example of this occurred in late 1975, when the PLP witnessed a confrontation between Stevie Coughlan and the leadership which involved basic questions of party loyalty. On that occasion, Coughlan argued that because a decision had been made to hold the party's annual conference in Dun Laoghaire rather than in Limerick (where his son was Mayor), his constituency delegation would not be coming to conference, and would probably be witholding national collection funds as well. If any of this meant that the Left swamped the platform, he said, it wouldn't be his fault, but the fault of a 'clique' which had 'rigged' the AC. To his credit, Corish took him on immediately, indicating that Coughlan's duty to conference was to make sure that his delegation was present, challenging him to be more specific in his allegation about 'cliques', and warning him that if he planned to carry out his threats about finances, the AC would obviously have to take some remedial action. Like many flare-ups of this kind, the matter ended without any rupture and the threat, if it was a threat and not a bluff, was withdrawn, but the exchange helped to bring into sharp focus the extent to which, even by that stage, the party had become sensitive to the pressure which could be exercised by its more conservative members. One of the chief peace-makers during this period was Brendan Halligan. Halligan believed—and still believes—that one of the major problems facing Labour is that, given the party strength, it has almost never achieved more than one TD per constituency. This has meant, especially outside Dublin, that the constituency organisation and the TD have become synonymous. Axe the TD on ideological grounds, and you have also lost an entire constituency organisation—and the votes which they can bring to conference to support a beleaguered leadership. Anybody who doubts this power should be in attendance in the seventies and early eighties. Frequently at conference—before registration formalities were tightened up to prevent the undignified scrum that used to ensue—it would be possible to see despots like Coughlan or Michael Pat Murphy paying delegate fees, and all the arrears of affiliation fees due by branches whose existence in non-election years was always a matter for conjecture, from immense wads of notes produced with a flourish from back pockets—and woe betide any hapless party official who queried any of the delegates' credentials. It was common, indeed, for more radical urban delegates to sneer, rant, or scoff at this human equivalent of ballot-stuffing, but in the final analysis the rural comrades' ability to deliver both conference delegates and general election votes in the appropriate numbers was something which their critics were rarely able to emulate. A person with a Dail seat, however acquired, speaks with some kind of authority, no matter how deficient his ideology may be.

At the PLP meeting just mentioned, Brendan Halligan went

so far as to say—ironically in view of his later convictions—that if he had his way conference would never be held in Dublin, where the organisation of the party had been subverted and taken over by people like Dermot Boucher (later SLP) and his allies, and that every 'header' in the capital would be present in the conference hall at Dun Laoghaire. Even Jimmy Tully, not noted for his radicalism, was to remark later that it was a very serious judgment to make on the party to say that it couldn't hold a conference in Dublin.

If there is one critical area in which the influence of the rural TDs and their organisations has been paramount, it is finance. Ever since its foundation, the Labour Party has been strapped for money, trying to raise election funds on a much smaller membership base to compete politically with two considerably larger organisations. Not only are these two organisations larger to begin with, but they also have fewer ideological difficulties about appealing, for example, to private industry for subventions.

This is not to say that Labour foregoes such appeals on grounds of principle: in fact, routine appeals for finance are made by the Labour Party to business organisations, both nationally and locally, even though it is fair to assume that the scale of generosity from such sources is, in the case of Labour, markedly less generous than it is to the other two parties. As in the case of the other two parties, the exact identity of donors to the Labour Party's funds remains confidential, and in the past at any rate confidentiality was generally understood to be a condition of the gift. In Labour's case, additionally, there was always an express condition that there would be no political kick-backs for any donation received. Whether corporate donations are actually critical to the financing of the party or not is a moot point. If they are particularly low, it might be better to stop looking for them, and to make a virtue of necessity, attacking at the same time the other two parties for the deals that may or may not be done behind the voters' backs. It is certainly true, at least, that proposals I have made from time to time to require corporate bodies to publish details of their political donations have excited little enthusiasm and much hostility. One of the problems that arose for the Labour Party in this area in the mid-1970s, for example, related precisely to the need for confidentiality. Michael O'Leary, the financial secretary at the time, raised in excess of £10,000 for the 1977 elections from certain donors on a basis so confidential that no-one other than himself knew the source, and the disbursements from this fund were made—in at least one case of which I am aware—by his own personal cheque.

One way or another, the Labour Party will not stand or fall on the basis of corporate donations. More critical are branch and constituency affiliations, and individual membership fees, all of which are set by conference and are actually enshrined in the party's constitution. This has created a phenomenon in which—again as an example of the model in which the periphery of the party dominates the centre—an impoverished central administration is supported by a national organisation which hoards its wealth and refuses to surrender it except at the point of a gun, i.e. when it comes to the time to register branch delegates for conference every year.

The AC report to conference for 1955–56 bemoaned the fact that branch affiliation fees to the party had not increased 'since the inception of the party'! And there is not much evidence that the situation has improved dramatically since then, as each successive revision has to be pushed through a party conference dominated by the people who have always resisted paying. Even in the 1977–81 period, when the party leader enjoyed a considerable amount of goodwill across the PLP as a whole, opposition from some rural deputies—notably Joe Bermingham, the PLP chairman—helped to stymie a proposal to increase branch affiliation fees to a realistic level. Even before this, Jimmy Tully had tried at conference—but less successfully—to have the affiliation fee for individual members abolished when it stood at only £1. If Irish political activists have been accustomed to getting their politics on the cheap, this is doubly true of the Labour Party, and especially of its non-urban supporters. This is in marked contrast to the Workers' Party, whose political professionalism extends to assuming that their membership will pay each year a sum roughly equivalent to the cost of union dues—which can go over £100 in some cases. Even at the present rate of £6 per year, this means that the average Labour Party member is acquiring his membership for less than two and a half pence a week.

The reference to the 'average' Labour Party member is, however, somewhat misleading, because the profile of the membership, as submitted by branches to Head Office, is somewhat unique. The reason for this is that there is a special low-level membership affiliation fee of £2 for unemployed members, young members, and old age pensioners, and members in these categories form an unusually high proportion of the total membership outside Dublin—if one is to believe the figures.

In 1985, for example, 332 of the party's 441 branches were located in Leinster and Munster. But an astonishing percentage of their 4027 members were registered as coming into one of these three categories—58 per cent in the case of Munster members, and an even more remarkable 63 per cent in the case of members registered for the greater Leinster area. By contrast, only just over 35 per cent of the Dublin membership were returned by their branches as fitting into these categories. One constituency registered no fewer than 78 per cent of its members as unemployed—another, only 21 per cent.

There is absolutely no way in which—even on the basis of other figures available to the party—these percentages are correct. But equally there is no way in which Head Office can disprove them, and so this transparent device for enabling some unscrupulous constituency organisations to register their members at a bargain-basement price, irrespective of their actual status, enables them, in effect, to buy votes an annual conference for a third of the cost borne by the more honest branches.

The same pattern is evident when one looks at the branches which are registered at the 'minimum' level, i.e. branches which have as few as five (rural) or ten (urban) members. Outside Dublin, 38 per cent of the branches are registered at the minimum level: in Dublin the figure is only just over 23 per cent. When it is remembered that each branch at the minimum level of enrolment is entitled to send two delegates to conference, the extent of the disparity can be clearly seen.

It is also the case that branches frequently concern themselves only with fulfilling the minimum conditions necessary for registration, particularly if the chief purpose of forming a branch is not to evangelise the locality but to ensure that four votes will be cast in a certain way at the next selection conference in the constituency. This is because no branch, no matter how large it is, can send more than four delegates to such a vital occasion.

The significance of this tactic for the financial health of the party organisation as a whole can be seen from the fact that branch affiliation and membership fees account for only about a quarter of the party's annual £125,000 (1985) income, with the national collection accounting for another quarter, the trade unions for a third quarter, and the PLP and other sources accounting for the final 25 per cent. The national collection is taken up during a specified period each year, usually in the spring, and each branch is required to return a minimum national collection (£175 in 1985) in order to qualify its delegates to vote at annual conference and at selection conferences. As is frequently the case, the minimum becomes—for many branches—also the maximum. Anything collected above the minimum figure is kept under local mattresses, to be used for branch or constituency purposes rather than for building up the party nationally. And some constituencies, and branches, can be relatively wealthy. The Kildare constituency, for example, owns a building in Naas which is rented out as offices. This rather extraordinary activity on the part of a socialist party can be explained simply enough: it was originally the property of former party leader William Norton, who left it to his local constituency organisation when he died. It did not, indeed, fall into the party's hands immediately, and legal action had to be taken before it did so, but it now provides an immensely valuable asset from which elections and other activities can be at least partially bankrolled. There are signs that some urban constituencies, at least, are moving rapidly into the twentieth century in financial terms. The turnover of the Dublin South-East constituency, for which Ruairi Quinn is the sitting Labour deputy, was of the order of £13,000 in 1985 (it was also, interestingly, the constituency to respond most positively to the party leader's request, late in 1985, for people to fill out bank standing orders to build up an election fund for the party as a whole).

The combination of the fact that the majority of Labour TDs come from outside the greater Dublin area, and the parsimony of their organisations towards the party's central office, greatly strengthens their independence of the party as a whole, in policy as well as in organisational terms. Nor do they, on occasion, trouble overmuch to hide the fact. In 1969, an order went out from the Administrative Council, flushed with the thought of impending victory, to the effect that there were to be at least two candidates in every constituency, even in those constituencies where sitting Labour TDs had become virtually part of the furniture, and where there was no constituency rival to be seen for miles. Different rural TDs handled this threat to their autonomy in different ways. Michael Pat Murphy, in West Cork, held two selection conferences in obedience to the instructions from Dublin. For some unaccountable reason, however, no other person offered himself or herself as a candidate, and Michael Pat ran on his own—and won. The authenticity of this process can be gauged from the fact that the constituency concerned, Cork South-West, which had eleven branches in 1981, had shrunk to two branches with a grand total of fifteen members in 1985—and this in a constituency which had had a Labour TD without interruption for half a century!

Later, during the 1977–81 Dail, there was an occasion on which the standing of various members of the PLP in relation to their monthly 'sub' to Head Office (then £20 a month) was detailed at a PLP meeting by assistant general secretary Seamus Scally. This was always the last item on each PLP agenda, but for some inscrutable reason was rarely reached. On this occasion, however, the list was read out in all its glory. Quite a few members were in arrears, but mostly by trifling amounts. Alphabetically, Spring's name was read out last, together with the fact that his indebtedness to the party coffers was numbered not in tens, but in hundreds of pounds (I believe that he refused to pay this—essentially voluntary—levy for many years on some point of principle). Spring was not actually present at the meeting, but in the hushed silence that followed this announcement Frank Cluskey's voice could be heard from his favourite vantage-point at the bottom of the long table, 'Spring, having exceeded the quota, is declared to be elected. . . . '

The problem is not only one of a dominance by the rural section of the party, but of the emergence and growth of a pattern of electoral independence between Labour and Fine Gael in the years since 1973. It is almost as if, after twelve years of abstention, the electorate plunged back into the joys of proportional representation with renewed commitment. That pattern is now responsible for the fact that a number of Labour seats, not least in the rural areas, are dependent on Fine Gael transfers to a degree that is positively alarming. In all the circumstances, it is perhaps to be expected that deputies like John Ryan do not go to inordinate lengths to highlight ideological differences between themselves and Fine Gael. In the 1977 election, for example, one of Ryan's campaign posters was adorned simply by a large picture of the candidate and his name, and the simple but effective slogan: 'THIS MAN GETS THINGS DONE!' There was no mention of the Labour Party.

The political freelance activities of a number of rural Labour TDs, on the other hand, never prevented them from invoking party policy—or what they believed to be party policy—when it involved their toes being trampled on. There was a case in point in 1976, when Brendan Halligan, not long after his by-election victory in Ballyfermot and a TD instead of merely general secretary of the new party, made a controversial speech on the economy. For this he was roundly abused at the PLP, especially by Stevie Coughlan, and Jimmy Tully suggested at one point that controversial speeches by PLP members should be cleared in advance—a proposal that was abandoned when it became clear what political and administrative chaos it would provoke. Going for a second bite, Tom Kyne then—unwisely, as it turned out— had a go at Conor Cruise O'Brien for a speech he had recently made to the Irish Humanist Association, which had also got widespread publicity. Conor, however, was better prepared: not only had he shown his speech to all the other Labour ministers, but he was stating official party policy.

The dominance of the rural constituencies within the party does not indicate a high level of organisation generally. In fact, of the fifteen or so constituencies in which Labour is currently either bereft of any organisation or where its organisation is too weak to carry out all but a partial election campaign, only three are in Dublin (Dublin Central, Dublin North-East, Dublin West). All the others are outside—a litany of areas which have been all but written off, even though in some cases they returned Labour deputies with apparently healthy votes: Roscommon (which returned Jack MacQuillan, no rural conservative, but for another party), Donegal South-West and North-East, Mayo West and East, Cavan–Monaghan, Galway East, Sligo–Leitrim, Cork South-West, East, and North-West, and Limerick West.

The division between urban and rural deputies is exacerbated by the fact that as the Workers' Party (and indeed Sinn Fein) grow in strength in the urban constituencies, their votes—where they are weaker than Labour—will tend to transfer to Labour in respectable numbers, making Labour in the city less dependent on Fine Gael votes. In such a situation, the tension between rural deputies becoming even more dependent on Fine Gael, and urban deputies and candidates becoming less so, could well threaten party unity in a way that has not been seen before.

The received wisdom among some sections of the Labour Left, especially in Dublin, is that hewing to a more socialist policy (which in practice means denying Fine Gael the chance of future coalitions) would result in a massive increase of Dail seats for the party. The difficulty about this is that with relatively few exceptions (Mervyn Taylor, for instance) the safer Labour seats are those which are held by the more conservative members of the PLP. In other words, a general decline in Labour's vote, spread evenly across the constituencies, will actually leave its Dail representation marginally more conservative than heretofore. At the same time, even an increase in its urban vote might not compensate, in terms of seats gained, for the seats that would be lost in the rural areas. The rural TDs had their Armageddon in 1969: they are not likely to want to repeat the experience if they can avoid it.

Much of the effort of the party leadership in the past ten years or so has been precisely aimed at preventing any split in the party between its rural and its urban standard-bearers. There are a number of circumstances in which a split might come about, and one of the most obvious of them would be if, in a post-election situation, a number of the more conservative Labour TDs decided to flout a conference decision on coalition and help to form a government to keep Fianna Fail out yet again.

It could happen. And the likelihood is that if it did happen the 'dissidents' would actually form a majority of the PLP, not only leaving the party irreparably split, but leaving it split in such a way that the conservative breakaway actually took the bulk of the party with it, rather than a minority. Minor breakaways can be contained: the case of Sean Treacy in Tipperary South is an example of how this can happen without too many reverberations beyond the obvious one caused by the loss of a seat. But it can be argued that the only split which might make sense in the Labour Party would be one in which the breakaway group was not only more conservative, but smaller, than the group left behind.

In any case, suggestions that a split is the answer to its problems is to betray a degree of desperation. And it ignores the depth and power of the folk memory, not only in the Labour Party but in the labour movement as a whole, of the damage done to socialism in Ireland by the deep divisions of the 1940s, which hit Labour just as it looked likely to take off politically in a way in which it had never done before.

For as long as the very existence of these deputies is perceived to act as a brake on the ideological progress of the party as a whole, and on its electoral success in the larger urban areas, this tension will remain. It will probably be solved in the long run only by growing urbanisation of the areas outside Dublin, and by the emergence in the party in these areas of more radical people who are dissatisfied with the staid politics of their predecessors.

5

Divided We Stand: Party Structures

THE BEST vantage point for watching a Labour Party Conference —that key element in the Labour Party's structure—is from the platform itself. This is not just because it affords the best view of the audience, or even the chance of appearing, however blurred and fleetingly, on television. One of the rarest insights it offers is a view of the party leader from behind, as he delivers his annual address to the faithful, *urbi* if not exactly *orbi*.

Each leader has his own characteristic style on such occasions. For Brendan Corish, for example, it was the opportunity to shed the diffidence which appeared at times to characterise him, or at any rate to transmute it into assertiveness and attack. The occasion on which his speech slipped to the floor and was handed back to him with the pages irretrievably mixed up would have tested a lesser man. His successor, Frank Cluskey, would appear to the television cameras and the public with no visible sign of tension other than a traditionally hunched shoulder; but below podium level, out of sight, a tapping foot or a whitening of the knuckles would signify the approach of a particularly thorny passage. Michael O'Leary's nervousness betrayed itself in the rapid aside to the general secretary, the quick stab at the glass of water, the hand brushing the hair back from the forehead. Dick Spring, by contrast, is virtually immobile—a fact related to his physique rather than to his temperament. On occasion he has had to use a special stool for support to alleviate the pain of a back injury which can become excruciating after standing for any length of time. When that stance is being maintained in front of an audience whose readiness to listen is often tinged with scepticism, and sometimes with downright hostility, all nerves and sinews have to do double duty.

Leadership, despite the air of omnipotence with which it is

sometimes endowed, is a much more provisional and tentative affair than is generally supposed, not least in the Labour Party. Most leaders in recent times have risen to address conference knowing that they have to address not one but three constituencies simultaneously: the television audience, the platform party (which will contain an indeterminate number of people who think they can do the job better than he can), and the rank and file immediately in front of him. And the decisive importance of conference, on occasions like this, can never be underrated. If a leader can carry conference, he has an immeasurably strengthened hand in dealing with the inevitable rivalries and bickering of the Administrative Council and the Parliamentary Labour Party. Without that sanction, as Michael O'Leary discovered to his cost, his grip on the leadership will weaken and probably slip completely. This is the reason why party leaders who know their business, who want to maintain their footing on the political greasy pole, have continually to fine-tune their appeal to this large and heterogenous group of people whose sole defining point of commonality is their membership of the Labour Party, and who represent local organisations of widely varying coherence and electoral significance.

Like the 'leaders of thought' in a West African village, political activists in Ireland play a social and political role that is not hallowed by statute but can be out of all proportion to their apparent strength. They are far from numerous. It has been estimated that no more than about 2 per cent of the population take an active part in representational politics between elections. Even at election time, that figure is thought not to rise above 4 per cent. Actual Labour Party membership is no more than about 5,600, and the disposition of this membership mirrors the disposition of the Labour national vote: only about 1,400 of the total live in the Dublin area. So active political engagement is a minority sport at the best of times: this does not mean, however, that it is not played with determination and sometimes with ferocity. It is also true that some of the most ferocious battles are internal ones, waged against one's own opponents in the party, in the name of principle, electoral advantage, or—happiest of all—both.

A classic example of this—and it could be replicated in many other constituencies, and in many other parties—was in the 1969 election in the Dun Laoghaire–Rathdown constituency, when

Barry Desmond and Flor O'Mahony were both battling for a Labour seat. Barry Desmond won the seat by some 300 votes, indicating that the battle might easily have swung either way: but before the votes were tallied, both sides broke just about every rule in the book in an effort to stay ahead, as a subsequent report by the director of elections showed.

At one stage in the campaign, Barry Desmond issued some 500 personalised leaflets: Flor O'Mahony retaliated with 5,000. This resulted in an agreement to issue no further personal literature, but a couple of weeks later several thousand cards bearing Barry Desmond's unmistakable features, and innocent of any reference to other party candidates, mysteriously appeared. One personalised canvassing team met in the hinterland of the constituency but the director of elections had not only failed to contact the ward director of elections, but appeared to be lost and was seeking directions from a prominent member of the Fianna Fail party. The director's report to the election committee subsequently spoke scathingly. of 'teams of mercenaries recruited from outside the constituency' who 'displayed the utmost contempt for the official party organisation'. One candidate alleged that another had instigated a rumour to the effect that he was a Communist, and the director's final comment was to the effect that Labour 'should be less ready to criticise Fianna Fail tactics while it contains within its own ranks individuals as well versed in the arts of political in-fighting as M/s. Boland and Blaney'.

The activists are important, and not only because they can make or break leaders. They decide, within certain broad limits, who will and who will not present themselves to the electorate as Labour Party candidates (and how). And, in a myriad resolutions, amendments, committee documents and working parties, they give shape to the countless policy statements to be directed, more in hope than in anticipation, at their small and harrassed band of public representatives. These activists, and the political structures within which they operate in the Labour Party, represent—and not only for party leaders—an abiding and significant political reality. Some of them come into the party less through ideological conviction than out of a kind of gratitude for constituency work well done on their behalf. Their decision to support their local Labour public representative may be political in character, or it may be related, more basically, to the degree to which he shows the flag on their

Three of the figures who dominated the party for most of the 1970s: Brendan Corish, the leader for seventeen years, seen *(above)* with Conor Cruise O'Brien, the intellectual stormy petrel of the party, and Justin Keating (centre, *right)*, the Minister for Industry and Commerce in the Cosgrave coalition, whom many on the left of the party saw as Corish's natural successor.

Noël Browne being set upon by police dogs outside the US Embassy in October 1962, at the time of the Cuban missile crisis.

Jimmy Tully, probably the most influential conservative in the higher echelons of the party during the 1970s. He was Minister for Local Government in the 1973–77 coalition.

The first parliamentary party meeting following the general election of 1982. Michael Bell is shaking hands with another new TD, Frank Prendergast of Limerick. Standing on the left of the photo, about to shake Bell's hand, is Mervyn Taylor. On the extreme right, Sean Treacy sits alone. He has since left the party and become an independent.

Two scenes outside the Gaiety Theatre in June 1981, immediately prior to the special delegate conference at which the party decided to enter into coalition on the terms negotiated by Michael O'Leary. Dick Spring *(above)* is getting on with the old style by making sure that all the North Kerry delegates have their admission tickets. Meanwhile a young member of the Militant Tendency *(right)* naturally takes a more ideological view of things.

The Gaiety conference duly approved O'Leary's plans and thus led to the formation of the first Garret FitzGerald coalition. The photograph above shows O'Leary receiving his ministerial seal of office from President Hillery. The photograph below shows him in more sombre mood, however, as the left of the party carry one of the crucial votes at the annual conference of October 1982. As a result of this conference, O'Leary resigned the leadership and joined Fine Gael.

Prior to the O'Leary interlude, the party had been led by Frank Cluskey (*left*), seen here watching his disappointing election result at the count centre at Bolton Street in June 1981. It was the lack of a safe seat that lost Cluskey the leadership. The photograph below shows the current leader of the party, Dick Spring, who was catapulted into the leadership in the wake of the O'Leary debacle, addressing the annual conference of 1985.

Labour is both an independent political party and an element in the greater labour movement. The photograph above shows two of the party's leading figures, Michael D. Higgins and Brendan Halligan in the company of John Carroll and the late Michael Mullen of the ITGWU on the occasion of a Labour Youth march against unemployment in 1981. Despite inevitable tensions, relations between the party and the unions remain close. Ruairi Quinn and Christy Kirwan (below) are shown here having an earnest tête-à-tête.

The spectacular growth of the women's movement in Ireland has naturally made itself felt in the party, and has found concrete expression in the Labour Women's National Council. The photograph above shows two of the LWNC's most influential members, Mary Robinson and Eithne Fitzgerald. The photograph below, taken at the LWNC's annual general meeting of 1986, shows Niamh Bhreathnach, the chairperson, with the party leader Dick Spring.

behalf. Thus, for example, Justin Keating's loss of his seat in the 1977 election may be put down, in large part, to the perception by many party workers in his constituency that he had physically abandoned them. Keating thought that by getting an extremely hard-working and efficient secretary to look after his constituency business when he was a minister, the honours would be sufficiently done. But the constituency activists do not want just service: they want the physical presence of their public representative, and they take it out on him or her fiercely if this is not delivered. Task forces sent out from Head Office into Keating's constituency during that election campaign returned like people who had stared death in the face: they had never seen a constituency organisation so run down, so helplessly enfeebled. And the conventional wisdom is that, by not looking after his own, Keating had sealed his fate. How much it squares with the reality—there were undoubtedly other factors operating which would help to explain his loss of popularity—is almost beside the point. The official moral is: you neglect your constituency party at your peril.

One interesting fact is that—in sharp contrast to the practice followed in the Workers' Party, for example—there are few, if any, tests for membership. The party constitution states that 'any person who subscribes to the Principles and Objects of the Party, accepts its Constitution and is not a member of any other political party or of an organisation subsidiary or ancillary thereto, may be accepted as an individual member of the party.' It goes on to note that 'an individual member must sign a declaration of adherance (sic) to the Principles and Objects and of submission to the Constitution and Standing Orders of the Party.' Few if any members sign any such declaration, or even receive a copy of the Constitution, must less of the Standing Orders. Fewer still, one suspects, have read either. Here, as in a number of other areas, there seems to be a wariness about implementing the Constitution in its fullness because of a fear that intending members would suddenly take fright and disappear over the horizon. There are few enough of them in captivity, after all. Coupled with this attitude is a certain reluctance to go out and hunt for members in ways the other parties have perfected. There is, almost, a feeling that Labour will attract people into its ranks by sheer political magnetism. Anyone who has watched Fianna Fail politicians in action at university meetings, for example, will observe how the brighter student speakers are flattered into believing that a decision by them to join Fianna Fail could not but be mutually advantageous. Even committed Labour members seem more hesitant in an area in which they have more to offer, but perhaps the continual rebuffs by the electorate have engendered a sort of private defeatism in this important area.

The Constitution of the party stipulates that members of the party must be either on the rolls at Head Office (a rare, and usually temporary arrangement), or in a branch 'in the Dail constituency in which he or she resides, or is registered as a Dail elector' (3.2.a). In some areas, notably in Dublin, this stipulation was widely flouted, as TDs and would-be TDs drafted in supporters from other areas to strengthen their bailiwick support. When Dublin Central was reorganised in the 1984–85 revision of party structure carried out by the AC, all the branches in the constituency had to be dissolved and re-formed. Close examination of the files revealed, for example, one ITGWU official, a member of a centre city branch, dating from Michael O'Leary's time, who lived not only in another constituency some fifteen miles away but almost in another county.

Some city centre branches continued to flourish and grew even as the physical environment they were alleged to be serving slowly disintegrated. The Cuffe Street branch of the party, for example, was a hotbed of left-wing subversion and dissension throughout the sixties, as the houses around the area tumbled to make room for office blocks. By the time it disappeared, its membership lived almost entirely in the suburbs, and the branch itself was more a PO box for dissidents than an organisational unit in the strict sense of the word.

The process of reorganisation is not without pain, and the toes that are trodden on can sometimes be very gnarled indeed. In the Dublin Central reorganisation, for instance, the Marino branch was amalgamated with a number of other branches to form a new centre city branch. Denis Larkin, who had been a TD in the area, complained bitterly at the time that there had always been a Marino branch: local loyalties die hard.

The converse of the situation in which the membership's ideological or residential qualifications were not too closely scrutinised was the problem created by barons who became so locally powerful that they preferred their constituency organisation to be totally under their control. In John O'Connell's Ballyfermot, for example, well-meaning Labour supporters were heard to complain at times that it was actually impossible to join the party. The same was to some extent true of West Cork, whose branch organisation was also totally dissolved in the 1984–85 period. In fact, one of the anomalies of the party's structure at present is that a person who wants to join a local branch of the organisation actually has no redress if refused admission, even though the reasons may have more to do with a local despot's desire to keep his power-base intact than to any real or imagined deficiency in the applicant. The applicant may appeal to Head Office, it is true: but Head Office's only remedy is to consult with the local organisation—which is where the problem arose in the first place. In the constituencies mentioned above, and perhaps elsewhere as well, this gap has contributed significantly to the erosion of Labour support.

Political organisation, the conventional wisdom goes, helps to deliver local authority and Dail seats into the hands of political parties. Branch and constituency officials, in particular, tend to elevate this to the status of dogma, usually to remind a party's elected representative that he or she holds office, not at the pleasure of the electorate, but at that of the party's faithful followers. All parties, therefore, tend their organisations with care. The difference between the Labour Party and the other major parties is that whereas the latter have traditionally taken precautions to prevent their organisations having very much to do with the formulation or execution of policy, Labour's devotion to the practice of internal democracy at all levels has at times achieved truly heroic—some would say suicidal—proportions.

A classic example of this was the procedure devised for the consideration of policy documents in a number of important topics, such as health, the economy, and planning, in the 1977–81 period. Before commonsense eventually prevailed, the party was faced with the prospect of having the entire conference discuss and amend these documents on a line-by-line basis, with each branch entitled to submit amendments as it chose! The party could have hardly chosen a better way to clog an agenda, and to make it virtually certain that the whole proceedings would become, as far as the general public was concerned, an excruciating bore.

There seems to be, in Irish politics, almost an inverse ratio between the size of any political party and the degree of sophistication of its organisation. Although Labour is the smallest of the three major parties, it is organised, both vertically and horizontally, to a degree that has been in the past (and can still occasionally be) an administrator's nightmare. Overall, it is governed by a constitution, which sounds commonplace enough. In recent years, however, the Constitution has risked becoming a battle-ground for opposing groups within the party, or at the very least fertile territory for the barrack-room lawyers who are to be found in every political party and for whom nothing is as enjoyable as amending constitutions. It is not that there is anything inherently wrong in amending a party constitution: but the danger is that it becomes a political activity in its own right, diverting considerable energies from the task of missionary activity among the heathen. This tendency is encouraged by the amount of detail contained in the Constitution, and by the fact that conference alone can amend it.

Conference is, under the Constitution, the supreme authority in the party. This is seen most dramatically in the way in which it is organised every year. In the major parties, all units of the organisation have the right to submit motions for discussion, but this is not to say that they all appear on the final agenda. In Fianna Fail, for example, the agenda is carefully chosen by the party bureaucracy, in close consultation with the front bench, to maximise the political and public relations impact of the conference as a whole. In the Labour Party, the agenda is a faithful—indeed a bewildering—reflection of the collective opinions of the membership, and the Standing Orders indicate quite clearly that every resolution and amendment must be disposed of in the traditional way, i.e. by a vote. A Committee on the reform of conference, which sat briefly and to some extent unavailingly in 1976, noted that the party was governed by an approach to conference which had taken shape when there were no more than 200 delegates and some 30 motions for discussion. Even at that stage, there were already an average of 200 motions from some 1,100 delegates and that there were not more was only due to a

104

voluntary limitation by branches on their right to submit motions. Originally each branch had the right to submit two motions. Each branch still has the right to submit one, and although not all branches take advantage of it, it is a mark of political virility among many of them to have their name on a conference agenda. The inevitable result is that debates become compressed to vanishing point, or run over, squeezing other subjects into even shorter time-slots; motions and amendments are inadequately discussed, and conference frequently takes decisions on matters of some substance without having had a really full debate—in some cases without having had any debate at all.

Conference, for example, cheerfully voted on one occasion to abolish ground rents, with compensation to be paid 'only in cases of proven need', to the horror of members of the PLP, who might sympathise with the sentiments but for whom Leninist expropriation is not the way forward in Irish electoral politics. Proposals to remedy this state of affairs provide a fair illustration of the encounter between the irresistible force and the immovable object. Branches, the PLP, and the AC are so fiercely attached to their democratic prerogatives that they will be slow, to put it mildly, to cede any of them for fear that the party bureaucracy, or 'Head Office' as it is contemptuously referred to on occasion— will acquire even more power.

The reality of the situation is, paradoxically, that failure to reform conference may have exactly the results feared by the activists: in particular, that a disputatious and unwieldy conference will be less and less regarded—except on really crunch points—by party officers and public representatives.

Many conference decisions turn on the votes of mandated delegates; indeed, part of the critical nature of branches derives from the 'mandate' system. At its most sophisticated, this system operates with all the precision of a Leningrad soviet. When it breaks down, it leads to intra-party recriminations which are little short of civil war. Under this system, the majority of branch members present at a meeting 'mandate' their delegates to vote in a particular way, or for a particular person, at annual conference or (especially) at a selection conference for election candidates. A scheme to improve the party's electoral performance by drawing up lists of potential candidates in each constituency (and in each ward for the local elections), which would have had the additional

105

advantage of preventing *coups* by power brokers at selection conferences, was first accepted by the AC, and then thrown out by the same AC when its implications for local power bases were suddenly realised.

There are, needless to say, occasions on which the delegate's personal views may well conflict with his or her mandate. If the ballot is a secret one, a mandate can be, and sometimes is, broken with impunity. This leads in turn to the unofficial adoption of procedures in which branch or constituency 'tellers' issue ballot papers to their members and collect them again, noting the way in which the votes have been cast. This practice is especially noticeable among some of the trade union delegations to annual conference, where a paramilitary discipline in voting procedures and outcomes can be observed. The ITGWU delegation to conference, for example, votes in just such a disciplined way during the elections for members of the AC, which are held in closed session at the end of every conference. If the Union has promised its votes to a particular candidate or candidates, it has to deliver.

In addition to the structural factors which condition the party's decision-making process, there are also functional and contingent ones. Of these, none is more important than the distinction which needs to be drawn between constituencies with sitting Labour TDs and those without.

Sitting TDs develop—it is human nature, after all—mechanisms to help them keep their seats. The first priority in keeping one's seat, under our PR system, is to ensure one's renomination. The second is to defeat the nomination of anyone from your own party on the same ticket who might conceivably threaten your tenure. This tends to produce, especially in those constituencies in which Labour seats are precarious (but not alone in these) a party philosophy which is always organisationally, and often ideologically, conservative.

Constituencies without sitting Labour TDs see the emergence of different aspirants, each followed by a team of people, one of whose functions is to make as much noise as possible on behalf of their candidate. In addition, frustration at the absence of political power inevitably leads individuals and units in this situation, kicking out wildly in an electoral vacuum, to adopt positions which can set the teeth of their elders on edge.

When Labour was in government in 1973–77, for instance, the

106

item 'correspondence', although rarely enough reached on the Parliamentary Labour Party agenda, would as often as not include a missive from some local branch or constituency council complaining about the party's actions in government and calling on the PLP to immediately create a socialist state or face the threat of mass defections or worse.

Into the pool of silence generally created by the reading out of such sentiments, Jimmy Tully's voice would drop with all the accuracy of a well-lobbed stone.

'Tell me', he would ask the general secretary, with an air of concerned and earnest enquiry which was betrayed only by the wolfish grin which accompanied it, 'Who is the TD for that constituency?'

As each branch sends delegates to a constituency council, and to selection conferences which nominate candidates for local and parliamentary elections, it represents a miniature power bloc. A would-be candidate needs to amass support from branches for his or her candidature: if there is no minimum stipulation for branch size, a political aspirant can spread his support like margarine around the constituency or ward. Politicians with an iron grip on their constituency organisations, therefore, are slow to accept changes which run the risk of concentrating their political support into unacceptably large, and possibly less predictable, units. They can be equally slow to accept gift horses. When the political climate within the universities in the 1960s and 1970s relaxed to the point where political parties could organise openly within them, a secondary problem arose: to which constituency—if any—would university branches be affiliated? Sitting TDs in constituency organisations whose internal politics were by now predictable were unwilling to introduce such wild cards into their packs: and on one occasion an energetic discussion between Conor Cruise O'Brien and Frank Cluskey about the optimum destination for the Trinity College, Dublin, branch (geographically in Cluskey's constituency), led to the then Minister for Posts and Telegraphs being told in abbatoir language exactly where to go. The following day, Cluskey received a letter from his adversary, noting that the advice tendered by him had been previously offered to O'Brien by a considerable number of people, beginning with U Thant, the secretary general of the United Nations, and ending 'last but not least', with Michael Mullen, general secretary of the Irish Transport and General Workers' Union.

107

By 1980, however, the situation had got to the stage at which something simply had to be done: the number of political rotten boroughs was becoming a cause for scandal. What was eventually worked out was, as so many of these things are, in the nature of a compromise. The minimum size for a 'rural' branch was set at five members; that for an 'urban' branch was set at ten members. In the discussions which took place on the issue in the parliamentary party and at the Administrative Council, the argument was made, especially by rural deputies, that maintaining the party presence in areas of scattered population was of vital significance, and that to set the minimum level for branch membership at too high a figure would be to condemn the party to extinction in many rural areas.

The compromise, therefore, was to set the minimum rural membership at five people per branch, and the minimum urban membership at ten per branch. As each branch with ten or fewer members is entitled to send two delegates to the party's annual conference, this means that whereas five rural members of the party control two votes at conference, it takes ten urban members to control the same number of conference votes. The other part of the compromise, however, laid down that for each additional ten members—a target harder for rural branches to reach—branches are entitled to an additional delegate to conference. The anomaly remains that in theory (and in fact) five rural members can have exactly the same voting strength at conference as fourteen urban ones. Even in a party which fought might and main for the retention of proportional representation, this example of positive discrimination is a matter for admiration.

It is worth noting, in passing, that party membership and party support are not always coterminous: in the 1977 election, party tallymen looking at the votes emerging from the polling station attached to a minuscule hamlet in the Wexford constituency noted with some consternation that the Labour vote in the box fell short even of the tiny number of registered party members in the village branch!

One of the reasons why this compromise secured adoption, it should be added, was the somewhat despairing realisation, on the part of the administrative council at least, that the overwhelming electoral strength of the party still lies outside the major urban areas. There was a distinct feeling, at the time the formula was being hammered out, that to go for the principle of one man, one vote, might be all very well in theory, but could have disastrous effects on party organisation in practice. The corollary of all this is that any move to change the system would have to get through a conference which is constructed under the old system; and examples of people handing over power gratuitously are hard to come by, above all in political parties.

There are several anomalies in the Labour Party structure, and one of them is the constituency council. This grand-sounding organisation has, between elections, relatively few functions to organise. It is charged, in a general way, with organising the constituency, and with raising finance for elections. It can set up branches in certain areas, but it cannot close them down: only the AC, effectively, has the right to do this. It can set financial targets for the branches, but it does not control branch finances. Although it may send a delegate to annual conference, that delegate is always outnumbered by the branch delegates, and the choice of delegate will reflect the existing power balance within the constituency. Recent constitutional changes have, in fact, given the AC an even greater oversight over branch organisation then heretofore, partly no doubt to deal with the 'paper branch' problem. Under these changes, every branch has to supply the AC (in practice, the general secretary) with the names and addresses of all its paid-up members, and the constitution now—with a marked absence of the comradely trust that used to characterise previous arrangements—notes that the AC 'may take whatever steps it considers necessary to verify the accuracy of the information supplied'!

———————

The AC is, along with conference and the PLP, one of the three key structures in the party, but its own composition is, as rank and file delegates have frequently complained, weighted to ensure that there are no sudden changes in the political direction of the party. Between conferences it is, according to the constitution, the body charged with 'the control of the organisation and the administrative affairs of the party.' The constitution also states—incorrectly—that the AC is 'elected at the annual meeting of the national conference.' In fact, only twenty of the thirty six members of the council are directly elected by and at the conference. In

109

recent years, moreover, constitutional changes have increasingly diluted the strength of the rank and file members of the party by first of all increasing the trade union representation from one to two, and then by adding in further reserved seats for representatives of the Labour Women's National Council and of Labour Youth, the party's youth organisation. Two people from the West of Ireland are usually co-opted—the practice is a bit like the Roman habit of appointing bishops to sees *in partibus infidelium*— but a further provision, allowing for the co-option of two more people from the party's organisation in Northern Ireland, is not implemented for the very good reason that the party does not maintain an organisation in the North, and has not done so for many years.

The emergence and growth of the women's and youth sections of the party, and their subsequent representation on the AC, while hardly unique in itself, has represented the party's structural response to the emergence of the women's movement and to the rapid growth in the youth population of the country.

The Labour Women's National Council was first established in 1975. Its current chairperson is Niamh Breathnach, a Dun Laoghaire teacher, and one of its most active members is Jean Tansey, also chairperson of the Divorce Action Group. In its early years it reflected an intense discussion that was then current in radical circles generally about feminism and socialism, and about which, if either, comes first. This, allied to a structure which envisaged that constituency delegates would travel to Dublin for regular Saturday meetings of the Council, tended to make it somewhat Dublin-dominated. Even in the Labour Party, perhaps, emancipation has not reach the point at which women members based outside Dublin are as free for weekend travel as their menfolk may be. Not surprisingly, the monthly LWNC meetings held under this structure rarely attracted more than twenty or thirty people. Up to then its main political activity involved canvassing for women at election times—and probably not very successfully at that. The organisational bias of the movement was reflected in what was the ~major achievement of that period—a well-researched document on equality, which betrayed one of its few blind spots by relegating the whole question of 'Rural Women' to a page at the very end.

In 1983, however, the Council adopted, with the support of the

AC, a new constitution which established an important network of regional and area sub-committees in an effort to dissolve the Dublin bias that had become apparent. The initial effects were, in a quiet way, substantial: regional meetings in places like Wexford and Cork not only indicated to women members of the party that they were more numerous than they had themselves imagined, but put their male fellow-socialists on notice that the women did not regard their political agenda as limited to questions of contraception and childcare. Its executive feels, moreover, that, in the words of Niamh Bhreathnach, members should put their main activity into the party at branch and constituency level, rather than into an organisation parallel to the mainstream.

The LWNC has, in effect, been the more successful of the two innovations mentioned. Women now represent just under a quarter of the total membership of the party, reaching a figure of 30 per cent in the Dublin region, and have their own organisation in twenty-seven of the forty-one constituencies. Not even this energy, however, has managed to make more than a slight dent in the trend of Labour Party membership, which is becoming increasingly male, and increasingly old, posing problems for replacement of the party activists that will be shown up with increasing clarity as the years elapse.

Labour Youth, on the other hand, is a different kettle of socialists entirely. Since the earliest attempts to found such an organisation within the structure of the present Labour Party, some fifty years ago, the very idea of a Labour Youth Movement has aroused mixed emotions. On the one hand it has been presumed that the very existence of such a movement will harness youthful energies for socialism with hitherto unimaginable success. On the other, the suspicion has been expressed that the young people will get out of hand, that they will not obey their elders and betters, and—worst of all—that they will be an embarrassment when the party is in government. Even in 1937, there was a row at the party's annual conference when the AC was accused—probably correctly—of foot-dragging on the issue. Defenders of the policy of procrastination tossed around thinly veiled rumours about the possibility of Communist infiltration.

Half a century later, with a Labour Youth Movement well established, the problem of infiltration has emerged in no uncertain manner. Since the early days of its existence in its

111

present form it has become a battle-ground between Militant and non-Militant members of the party and has, at the time of writing, been virtually colonised by the Militant group. The effects of this can be seen in the attenuation of the organisation. In 1980, for example, there were 140 delegates at Labour Youth's Annual Conference. In 1985 there were fewer than 100. The apparent decline in the appeal of this section of the party to young trade unionists was even more obvious: there were only three trade union delegates at the 1985 Labour Youth Conference. As a percentage of the total party membership, they number only 8 per cent, and the highest percentage is not in Dublin, as might be supposed, but in Connaught–Ulster. This may be explained in terms of the strength of Militant in the Galway West constituency, but whatever way it is explained, the figures are disheartening. At the same time, they do not necessarily reflect the reality of the situation in all its complexity. The fact that there is no necessary correlation between the strength of the Labour vote and the strength of Labour Youth, for instance, is possibly an indication that strong Labour TDs have actively discouraged the organisation in their own areas, knowing that its establishment would lead to internecine warfare and the emergence of a Militant takeover bid rather than to the growth of a healthy youth section. Thus, in Munster, Labour Youth accounts for only 5 per cent of the total party membership.

Two questions of a more fundamental nature can, however, be raised about Labour Youth. The first is the question of whether the young people who are initially attracted into its ranks are eventually disillusioned, not just with the mantra-like repetition of slogans and formulae, but with socialist politics altogether. If this is the case—and there are some reasons for supposing that it is—it represents attrition, with a vengeance, of one of the most valuable assets the Labour Party could hope to cultivate.

The second, more general point, is whether the creation of a separate organisation for young people within the party actually fulfils the political purposes originally outlined for it. It would certainly be wrong to try and maintain that this particular initiative has achieved, or even contributed significantly to, increased party support among young people. Indeed, the creation of Labour Youth has conspicuously not done anything to arrest the decline in the party's electoral fortunes, while at the same time it has saddled the party with two further organisational structures which need to be serviced from permanently inadequate resources.

A case could well be made out for the argument that the only positive gains from the setting up of Labour Youth were its initial public relations impact, and that it now tends to operate, within a party which already possesses an organisational structure of Byzantine complexity, as a further haemorrhage of scarce human resources—resources which should be integrated more fully into the parent organisation. There is even a certain inherent absurdity in allowing—even encouraging—people to remain in Labour Youth for eight years after they have acquired the right to vote in general elections. As things stand, Labour Youth now effectively has not only its own structures, organisation, and annual conference, but also—despite the fact that the many motions passed at the annual youth conference do not become party policy until they have been endorsed by the AC (an unlikely event)—its own policies.

In a much larger party, such organisational pluriformity might well be productive. In one as small as the Labour Party, it is certainly open to question. The probably insuperable problem, on the other hand, is how to overcome the institutional inertia which makes organisations, once created, highly resistant to change and almost totally immune to abolition. That being the case, Labour Youth is likely to remain part of the scenery for quite some time to come.

The filling of the Parliamentary Party seats on the AC is, theoretically, an elective process. Most frequently this was a mere formality: the party leader indicated to his colleagues at a meeting whom he proposed to nominate, and this generally did not evoke any discussion. Once during the 1977–81 period, however, Deputy John O'Connell demanded—and secured—an election, without actually managing to secure any change in the composition of the group of delegates formally proposed by the party leader. Parliamentary Party members of the AC, it must be said, are rarely conspicuous by their attendance, especially during the dog-years of opposition, as the party's annual reports clearly indicate, unless key questions concerning their interests are to be discussed. But they represent a powerful reserve army for the party leader to call on when the going gets tough.

113

The Parliamentary Labour Party (more generally known as the PLP), therefore, is the third leg of the tripod which—with conference and the AC—supports the overall Labour Party structure. It is, however, an entity which is not even mentioned, as such, in the party Constitution. It shyly pokes its head in here and there, and is referred to not as the PLP but variously as 'the Labour Party in the Oireachtas' and 'the Labour Party in Dail Eireann'.

The distinctions are important. The entire PLP including Labour Senators elects six members to the AC and jointly with the AC chooses Senate candidates to be supported by the party at election times. On the other hand, it is the Labour Dail deputies alone who have the power to choose the party leader and deputy leader.

Labour differs from, for example, Fianna Fail, Fine Gael and the Workers' Party in having a meaningful separation of powers. Side by side with the leader and deputy leader, elected by the Dail deputies, however few in number, there are the chairman and vice-chairman, elected by annual conference, which is ever more numerous. This is an organisational peculiarity which has created tensions in the past and may well do so again in the future.

Which is supreme, the PLP or annual conference? The party constitution implicitly favours annual conference, but perhaps wisely stops short of saying so in as many words. Only in relation to each party election programme, responsibility for which rests unambiguously with the AC 'in consultation with the Labour Party in Dail Eireann' (Article 9.3) is there any degree of clarity. It is altogether probable that, were it put to the test by conference making demands which a majority of the PLP was unwilling to accept, PLP members would claim that their mandate derived more from the electorate than from the party. Even at the present time it is not uncommon to hear PLP members, who have been ringingly instructed by conference to perform twenty-three impossible things before breakfast (conference is occasionally given to extravagant gestures, especially during the Sunday morning sessions when few but the enthusiasts are out of bed, mutter about the folly of expecting pigs to fly without wings. In practice what happens is that both conference and the AC accept, however grudgingly, that there are inevitable curtailments on the actual political power of a minority party, even in government, and that this is an unpalatable fact of political life.

Divisions at the 1985 Conference, for example, were particularly sharp on the question of the National Plan and on the vexed question of local authority charges. The agenda was littered with motions deploring the actions of the Labour Party in government. One, describing the actions of Environment Minister Liam Kavanagh as 'hypocritical', was passed, as were others calling for example on the PLP to ensure the 'immediate implementation' of transport proposals which the Plan had specifically rejected. Liam Kavanagh described what had happened as 'a bit of a cod', and it was equally certain that the National Plan would not be changed to meet the wishes of delegates. None of this, however, prevented the Conference from 'instructing' the PLP to perform tasks for which it does not have a numerical base in Dail Eireann: in the absence of a specific debate about coalition at that particular conference, the absence of the obvious sanction made such motions ring rather hollow. At the same time, senior party figures must be aware that a growing divergence between conference and the PLP, while perhaps clarifying the question of the PLP's large measure of autonomy, does not do much for party morale generally.

The crunch would come, it is safe to say, in a situation in which conference directed the PLP to withdraw from a government. Legally the PLP might not be bound to obey; politically it would find it very difficult not to. Whatever it did would involve the very real risk of a split party, with PLP members and activists on both sides. This is probably the main reason why such a confrontation has not yet happened. It is also the reason why debates on coalition at conference are 'real time' debates, in the sense that the decisions taken are operational in fact (whatever the constitutional theory) and not merely expressions of political opinion. The closest the party ever came to such a situation was when it rejected at conference the electoral strategy proposed by Michael O'Leary in 1981: the possibility of a split was averted on that occasion only because a compromise decision was arrived at which did not express a direct view on the thorny coalition question.

The PLP is therefore to some degree an independent republic within the party, in the sense that its ties with the party as a whole are primarily political rather than organisational. Its standing orders are its own creation and have never, to my knowledge, been written down in any codified form. New members are expected to learn them by watching them in operation, which can be extremely confusing at times, especially when it rapidly becomes obvious that there is no apparent limit on the number of times any member may speak on any issue, or when one encounters virtuosi like Stevie Coughlan or Michael Pat Murphy. During one particular meeting, one member, anxious to challenge a never-ending peroration by Michael Pat Murphy, felt his sleeve tugged by his neighbour, Conor Cruise O'Brien, who had noticed him getting ready to intervene.

'There is an old African proverb', O'Brien warned him sibilantly. 'Never get between water and the hippopotamus.'

The PLP likewise decides, in its own wisdom, the details of any election it chooses to conduct. When Frank Cluskey and Michael O'Leary received the same number of votes (eight each) in the leadership election of 1977, for example, normal proportional representation procedure would have indicated that the two names would be put in a hat, and one drawn out (the winner being the candidate whose name was *not* extracted). On that occasion, however, the procedure adopted, on Ruairi Quinn's suggestion, was the unusual one of a fresh ballot, which allowed one of those present (thought to have been Liam Kavanagh, but the person responsible has kept it to himself or herself, as the case may be) to change their ballot.

In much the same way, the PLP is the sole arbiter of its own disciplinary procedures, and is not answerable for them to any section of the party. This is apart from the 'party pledge' which is signed by all candidates for election, and which in its current form is modelled in part on that adopted by the old Irish Parliamentary Party at Westminster. This pledge, largely drafted by Conor Cruise O'Brien, is administered by the AC, not by the PLP. It contains an undertaking by each candidate to do a number of things, including an undertaking to resign his or her seat when called upon to do so by the AC. This pious aspiration has never been invoked—at least not in recent years—no doubt for the reason that it would have no effect whatsoever on the delinquent. When one considers that such delinquents in recent years have included people of the calibre of Dr John O'Connell, Mr Michael O'Leary, Mr Micky Mullen and Mr Christy Kirwan, the AC's decent reticence is easier to understand. Each of these people have lost the whip, or left the party, in circumstances in which their earlier signing of the party pledge might at least have been recalled to them. Two of them, Michael

116

Mullen and Christy Kirwan, were government-appointed Senators who voted against security legislation supported by Labour ministers and other Labour TDs and Senators. John O'Connell left the party when it refused to allow him to run in the area of his choice after constituency boundaries had been redrawn, and Michael O'Leary's defection to Fine Gael was perhaps the most spectacular abandonment of a burden which had been taken up so unambiguously. When Helena McAuliffe-Ennis left Labour for the Progressive Democrats, an attempt was made to embarrass her by calling on her to resign her seat: but it was an empty gesture, no more successful than the similar ones which were being made within Fianna Fail in relation to their defecting TDs.

During the long years in opposition up to 1973, discipline was a matter which presented Brendan Corish with many headaches. Free of the cares of government, many Labour parliamentarians simply went their own way. Whether Labour deputies ever actually turned up to vote in the Dail during those opposition years other than on the major occasions such as the Budget and the Adjournment was, despite Barry Desmond's best efforts as chief whip during the latter part of that period, essentially a matter for themselves. In government, naturally, things were more difficult. And the difficulties of the PLP were increased by the fact that under existing procedures withdrawal of the party whip (i.e. expulsion from the PLP, though not necessarily from the party itself) was a matter to be decided on its merits in each case. In other words, nobody could lose the whip without a vote and, in all probability, a tense and acrimonious debate into the bargain. The potential of this procedure for increasing the sense of strain in a body which was not in any case bound very tightly together can be imagined. Even on occasions on which there was a substantial majority in favour of withdrawal of the whip, emotions could run very high. The expulsion of David Thornley provided just such a mixture of emotion and high drama. What differentiated it from the general run of disciplinary problems experienced by the party in government is that it did not relate to a Dail or Seanad vote, but to what might, in Fianna Fail at any rate, be described as 'conduct unbecoming a member of the party'.

David Thornley, in some ways one of the most gifted members of the Parliamentary Party, had been a television current affairs commentator on 'Seven Days', one of the precursors of 'Today

Tonight'. Sucked into electoral politics in the heady atmosphere of 1969, he joined Labour and was elected for the Cabra area with considerable ease. It was, in effect, one of the few Labour heartlands in Dublin. When there had been only one Labour TD in the capital (Michael Mullen) this had been his constituency. The future for Thornley, who was also a Trinity don and a writer, looked set very fair.

The reality of Leinster House politics, however, combined with the grinding hopelessness of what seemed to be permanent opposition, tarnished Thornley's hopes and, eventually, sapped his stamina and his morale. A surprisingly mawkish and un-donnish speech—almost as if he was overwhelmed by the occasion— marked his first day in Leinster House, when he proposed Brendan Corish as Taoiseach. Thereafter, moments of brilliance, and of fun, began to give way to darker episodes. In particular Thornley, who was English-born although of Irish parentage, developed a love affair with Irish nationalism. This reached its apogee early in 1976 when David, partly in order to protest at a decision which he felt in any case had been unjust, sat on a platform during speeches given by Provisional Sinn Fein spokesmen after a banned rally. On 28 April, Brendan Corish proposed his expulsion for conduct which had been 'injurious to the party', i.e. his attendance at the banned march.

The PLP discussion was odd, to say the least. David played a tape of an RTE interview in which he had defended his decision and then said that he would leave the meeting in case he spoke about personalities and said things he might later regret. This statement of principle was inconsistent with an earlier remark in which he had said that Conor Cruise O'Brien would not be sitting in judgment on him if he had managed to 'wangle a professorship in Trinity or the director-generalship of RTE'!

The discussion after he left was low-key: everyone was conscious of David's illness—perhaps illnesses—and the strain under which he was working. The only really unexpected revelation, made after the vote by the PLP chairman, Tom Kyne, was that if the vote had gone against Brendan Corish's suggestion both Corish and Tully would have resigned their Cabinet positions. Subsequent to the Thornley case, the disciplinary procedure was refined on two occasions, with the overall objective of avoiding the spectacle of blood seeping out from under the door of the PLP rooms in the

1932 Annexe in Leinster House. The first change was made after Michael Mullen, general secretary of the ITGWU and a nominee of Brendan Corish, had voted against a Criminal Law Bill. This change was to ensure that anyone who voted in the Dail or Seanad to oppose any legislation brought in by a government which Labour supported would forfeit the whip automatically: no vote, no debate, no *angst* (or at any rate not very much). This tightened up the situation for a while, until the Criminal Justice Bill debate in the Seanad when a number of Labour Senators, myself included, realised that the PLP disciplinary code, newly minted though it was, did not make any mention of abstentions. The Senators who abstained on that occasion did so in the expectation that this loophole, too, would soon be stopped up. And so it was.

At a meeting in September 1976, Brendan Corish raised the question of abstentions but, surprisingly, did not at that stage propose any sanctions or indicate that there would be a tougher line in the future. Some of the members present were less reticent. One of them, Michael Ferris, was in favour of expulsion for abstentions: after the meeting, he told a colleague that the whip summoning him to the Seanad because some of the Labour Senators were planning to abstain had deprived him of attending one of the biggest days of his life—the twenty-first anniversary of the Bansha Agricultural Show! Stevie Coughlan, ever a racing man, accused the backsliders of betting with other people's money, and Frank Cluskey, too, suggested that the situation had only arisen because we had taken advantage of an ambiguity in the rules laid down after the Mullen affair. Some of the heat engendered in the discussion was directly related to pressure being felt by ministers: Jimmy Tully, in particular, made no secret of the way in which he and his family were being threatened (usually on the telephone) by Republican sympathisers with graphic descriptions of what would happen to them if this Bill was passed, and uttered sentiments about getting out of the kitchen if the heat was too great. Because no formal motion on discipline had been on the agenda, however, the whole matter was postponed to the 25 October meeting, when a resolution was put to, and carried by, the PLP in the names of Brendan Corish, Jimmy Tully, and Joe Bermingham. It laid down that 'any member of the PLP who abstains from supporting or who votes against the government, other than one which the PLP has decided not to support or to permit a free vote, shall automatically cease to be a member of the PLP upon that abstention or the casting of that vote and shall immediately forfeit the Labour whip.' The sting, however, was in the second part of the resolution, which noted that 'the PLP shall advise the AC not to ratify any person as a Labour Party candidate in a general election to Dail or Seanad Eireann from whom the PLP whip has been removed.'

The latter represented a real sanction, even though its terminology paid effective obeisance to the constitutional propriety that it is the AC, and not the PLP, which ratifies general election candidates. The power to withold ratification has been rarely exercised, but one of the most recent occasions on which it was parallel to the situation envisaged by this motion in that it related to Noel Browne, who refused to take the party whip rather than had it withdrawn from him.

The AC, without directly referring to Browne, passed a resolution which had the effect of preventing any party member in the Oireachtas who had refused to take the whip from standing as an official party candidate. The fact that there was only one target of this deceptively general instruction did not really fool anyone: Browne stood, ran, and got elected as an independent.

At the meeting at which this decision was taken, Justin Keating expressed the opinion that, were Labour in opposition again, discipline could be more relaxed. The four years of opposition which rapidly supervened bore out his contention to some degree. With no government likely to be imperilled by a Labour deputy's vote, the old disciplinary ethos was effectively restored. The absence of effective sanctions led to huge gaps on Labour Party benches when the division bells rang. Deputies would argue passionately with the whip that their presence in their constituency was incomparably more important than presence in the lobbies for a vote they knew would be lost in any case. The comparative lack of interest by the media in what was actually happening in the division lobbies—conditioned in part by the overwhelming Fianna Fail majority already referred to—was the party's salvation.

Only on some occasions did they pay attention—as, for instance, during the discussion and vote on the Labour Party attempt to set up an all-party committee on divorce, when high-grade arm-twisting ensured that none of the waverers—Dan

Spring, and Stevie Coughlan in particular—would actually vote against. In the event, the damage limitation technique ensured at least that the waverers tactfully absented themselves.

From time to time—as in the 1969 report on the reform of the party constitution—a strong case was made for having the party leader elected, from among the Dail deputies, by annual conference. The same report, incidentally, recommended the abolition of the six 'reserved' AC seats for PLP members: one wonders what its authors would have made of the way in which 'reserved seats' have grown rather than diminished in number in the intervening period. It is certainly foreseeable that this suggestion will be made again: had Michael O'Leary remained leader, it might have been made sooner rather than later. If it is made, however, two related problems will have to be addressed. One is that of whether such an election will make redundant, or at least reduce, the role of party chairman. The latter is certainly the case in Britain, where the Labour Party chairman has neither the political nor media stature that his counterpart has here. The second is that there is at least a theoretical possibility that the person chosen as leader by annual conference might not have the confidence of a majority of his Labour colleagues in Dail Eireann, thus making the job of parliamentary leadership more difficult, if not on occasion downright impossible. The difficulties some leaders, elected solely by their colleagues, have had in this regard is noteworthy. Either way, it is at least the case that leadership elections in the Irish Labour Party take place only in the wake of general elections, and not, as in Britain, potentially every year. The present separation of powers means, in addition, that every party leader, no matter how popular, has continually to bear in mind the balance of power between conference and the AC on one hand, and the PLP on the other. It is one thing to be aware of that balance of power: it is quite another to have to continually wage battles in order to maintain a leadership position and, in the final analysis, even winning those battles may not be enough.

121

6

United We Fall: Labour and the Unions

THROUGHOUT 1984 and into 1985, newspaper readers must have been puzzled by the regularity with which one trade union after another appeared to be on the point of severing its links with the Labour Party. In three of the major unions in particular—the Irish Transport and General Workers' Union, the Federated Workers Union of Ireland, and the Amalgamated Transport and General Workers' Union—the run-up to their annual conference would be punctuated by strident noises from branches demanding disaffiliation. The No. 2 Branch of the ITGWU, for example, stated in their resolution to the 1985 Conference, 'By their continuing support of the most anti-working class government in the history of this state, the Labour Party has shown it has nothing in common with the aims and aspirations of the trade union movement. We urge this union to disaffiliate from the Labour Party.' At conference time, however, the story was always the same. Delegates voted, with varying degrees of reluctance, to maintain their links with Labour in the hope that the party would mend its ways and in the hope that union influence on party policy would increase. As general secretary, Billy Attley of the FWUI told his own union's annual conference in May 1985, 'Rather than depoliticising our movement, we should be moving to strengthen our influence and ties with the Labour Party, for the trade union movement needs political support if it is to achieve all its objectives.' Still, there were tricky moments. Despite the opposition of its general secretary the union, on the very day on which he spoke, almost passed another resolution which would have caused organisational and political chaos. Defeated only by the casting vote of the chairman in an extremely depleted hall (124 votes to 124 was the actual tally), it proposed that 'monies from the political fund should not be granted to any prospective

(Labour) candidate who supports coalition with Fine Gael'!

Perhaps even more significantly, a speech on the thirty-eighth anniversary of James Larkin's death by the general president of the FWUI, Tom Garry, indicated in January 1985 that the whole question of the relationship between the two arms of the labour movement was not one that concerned solely rank and file dissenters. In his speech, Garry referred to one of Larkin's characteristics which is not often praised—his willingness, 'where he thought it necessary, even to break the movement's strength in any struggle that offered for workers a significant advance, always convinced that the movement would regroup and re-emerge even stronger and more determined than before.'

Garry failed to be more specific about what might have to be broken, but later in the same speech he warned, 'the time may not be far off when we in this movement may have to consider a plan of concerted action *of both political and economic measures* to halt this spiralling downward trend (of unemployment).' The 'political' measures he had in mind may well have included the possibility of his union, or a group of unions, launching a political party tied directly to the trade union movement and campaigning on a sharply limited number of issues, such as tax reform, unemployment and social welfare. It goes without saying that such an initiative, if it ever took place, would spell the death of the Labour Party in its present form, but the fact that such options are even being hinted at gives some indication of the seriousness with which the situation is viewed.

Some time after Garry's speech John Mitchell, general secretary of the Union of Distributive Workers and Clerks, actually articulated such a point of view directly, and circularised other unions to investigate the possibility of setting up a new party along these lines. His initiative fell on stony ground, and was repeated in another circular to 200 trade unionists in January 1986. But a similar initiative from a more broadly-based union, if it were ever launched in earnest, would undoubtedly cause a political earthquake.

Behind this she-loves-me-she-loves-me-not scenario are a number of political paradoxes which throw some of political Labour's endemic weaknesses into sharp relief. It is striking, for example, that although a higher proportion of the Irish workforce is organised in trade unions than in any other European country—

some 57 per cent—this high degree of unionisation coexists quite comfortably with a national vote for the Labour Party that has never exceeded a third of this figure. Even the most naive student of political science would raise an eyebrow at this negative correlation. It is all the more remarkable when we consider that the Irish Labour Party was originally a natural development from the trade union movement. The party's origins in 1912 were in the formation of a joint Trade Union and Labour Congress in Clonmel, and when the political side of the movement was established formally as a separate entity in 1930, the theory, at least, was that this would increase the effectiveness of both parts of the movement. Since then, however, while industrial labour's strength has grown, political Labour has never caught fire as a real force in Irish society. As John Kane, a leading official in the ITGWU and an unsuccessful Labour candidate in the local elections in 1969, told a meeting in early 1985, there are only 150,000 farmers, whereas there are some 600,000 trade unionists, and 'including wives and families, we probably command up to a million votes.' Even without hindsight, the use of the word 'command' can be seen to be inappropriate.

A related anomaly is the fact that all these Irish trade unionists, far from failing to support Labour because it is not socialist enough for them, actually support, in huge numbers, political parties which, to put it mildly, rarely take the side of organised workers. A recurrent theme in the speeches of some Fianna Fail and Fine Gael political figures, for example, has been to attack trade union leadership on the grounds that it is in some way subversive. George Colley, in 1979, was blunt about it, 'Workers must ask whether they are being manipulated by power hungry people whose ultimate aim is the destruction of the democratic system in this country'. This sort of smear was not new. And yet, it seems, for many trade unionists Fianna Fail is the chosen vehicle for their political protest, when it is expressed: one poll in April 1985, when the government was certainly far from popular, indicated that Fianna Fail could count on the support of 59 per cent of working-class voters. Even Fine Gael, which might be assumed to be more blameworthy for economic hardship in the eyes of Irish workers, could lay claim to 23 per cent of the working class vote—almost three times as much as the Labour Party's 8 per cent.

In the circumstances, it is perhaps hardly surprising that in 1980 the Fianna Fail Ard Fheis was actually opened in style by the Irish Transport and General Workers' Union brass band (an event which caused near-apoplexy among some dedicated Labour Party members of that union). Nor did the closeness of that union's organisational links with Labour prevent its then general secretary, Michael Mullen, from playing a key role in the labyrinthine negotiations between Mr Haughey and Tony Gregory in 1981 which helped to cement a precarious power-base for Mr Haughey's short-lived government. Equally, it is significant that Fine Gael has for some years carefully cultivated a 'Trade Union Group' which, although largely cosmetic, has a useful public relations function.

Both Fianna Fail and Fine Gael, of course, draw their political support across social class barriers, and hence it is important for each of them to maintain some level of identity with working-class priorities and aspirations. In this they are aided by the nature of the electoral system which, in large multi-member constituencies, allows such parties to put up candidates to appeal to different (and possibly even mutually antagonistic) social groupings. This enables them to maintain a grasp on the political loyalties of working-class people even at the most unlikely times. As Jimmy Tully complained mournfully in 1979, 'I hadn't been doing clinics before I became minister but after that I used to have fifty or sixty people in three clinics a week. It was galling to me to find on election day that people who had got a very good service from me went in to vote for Fianna Fail'.

Side by side with this is the fact that the nature of the links between the Irish Labour Party and the trade union movement is quite different from that obtaining in, for example, Britain. The difference is important because, in the cultural overspill from Britain that marks Irish politics in more ways than one, it can very readily be assumed, especially by East Coast residents with access to British television, that Irish trade union leaders wield the same sort of power in Irish Labour as their counterparts do across the Irish Sea. There, the spectacle of one person at a Labour Party Conference holding aloft a single slip of paper registering more than a million votes for or against a particular proposal graphically illustrates the power of the big battalions. Indeed, British trade unions control almost six sevenths of the total number of votes at the UK Labour Party Annual Conference, and individual trade unions control the nominations of parliamentary candidates to many traditionally safe Labour seats. This has never been the situation in Ireland, although in the past unions which had a traditionally strong relationship with the Labour Party might— even if they were not formally affiliated—be encouraged to expect that some assistance would be forthcoming for their parliamentary hopefuls in certain circumstances. Thus in 1947, for example, the Labour leader William Norton could write to unions seeking financial assistance, and add that if the unions to whom he was writing provided the names of those of their members who might be interested in nominations, 'we shall do our utmost to have them selected without delay for suitable constituencies.' (Letter to IWWU, 7 November 1947). He was careful not to promise what he could not deliver: then as now, the prerogatives of individual branches and individual constituencies were jealously guarded. And it is inconceivable that any Labour leader of today would write to a trade union in similar terms. In Britain, the trade union vote for conservative policies, while worryingly high in recent years, has never been the regular landslide which takes place at every Irish general election.

One key difference is in the nature of the relationship. In Britain trade unions can affiliate to the Labour Party at constituency as well as at national level. In Ireland, affiliation is only at the national level. As the party Constitution notes, 'Trade unions, professional associations, cooperative societies and other organisations, the objects and activities of which are recognised by the Administrative Council as consistent with those of the party may be admitted as corporate members of the party . . . corporate members must accept the Principles and Objects of the party and agree to conform to its Constitution and Standing Orders.' In the still-born 1969 attempt to re-organise the party's structures, particular initiatives which would have given the unions more formal power were resisted by—of all people, some might think— Young Jim Larkin, who perhaps had better reasons than most to be wary of some of the ways in which the power of those big battalions can be exercised.

The unions have not always acquiesced in the comparatively minor role they are allocated in the formal structures of the Labour Party. In the late 1970s, for example, the affiliated unions put down a resolution for annual conference urging that their representation on the AC, then standing at one member, should be increased to six. They then sought a meeting with the party leader, Frank Cluskey, to clarify his attitude to the proposal. Led by Michael Mullen, the delegation was told by Cluskey, with his usual bluntness, that he was prepared to recommend an increase in their AC representation to two seats, and if that was not satisfactory, they could take their chances with a resolution at conference.

Mullen and the others, skilled negotiators that they were, knew that the time for huffing and puffing was over: it would have been very hard for them to have carried their resolution at conference against the party leadership, and so, effectively, the choice they were being offered was an extra seat—or nothing. They accepted, and that was the end of it. Their representation on the AC, therefore, is no greater than that accorded to two numerically much less significant groups—the Labour Womens' National Council, and Labour Youth.

This limitation on trade union power within the Labour Party has a number of important side effects. It prevents, for example, the development of trade union control over the nomination of candidates for local and national elections. The party structure, based as it is on the individual member in the local branch, is all but invulnerable to organised takeovers of this kind—although individual TDs and councillors, once elected, generally use patronage to maximise their control over their own organisations. At least one recent general secretary, Brendan Halligan, was strongly opposed to any extension of trade union presence and power in such a vital area.

It also limits the influence of trade union delegations at annual conference, where they form maybe ten per cent of the total voting strength. The importance of this voting strength, however, is not that it can be used to dominate a conference (because it obviously cannot), but that when conference is finely balanced on some particular issue, the disciplined use of that relatively small bloc of votes can be of key importance. It can certainly help to ensure the election of trade union figures to the Administrative Council. More importantly, on substantive issues it can be absolutely crucial, as was dramatically shown during the 1985 Annual Conference in Cork. On the second day of that conference, there was a vote on a motion which would have committed the Labour Party in government to renegotiate the

National Plan—which all members of the PLP had voted for in the Dail—and to report on the results of that renegotiation to a special party conference in the autumn of the same year. That motion was defeated by only eleven votes—243 to 232—and a critical factor in its defeat was the decision by the ITGWU delegates, some seventy strong, to vote against it. John Carroll, president of the ITGWU, was a prime mover on this occasion, and evoked from *The Sunday Tribune* the observation that he was 'positively ingratiating even to the extent of voting obtrusively with the platform when it seemed as if they might be in trouble.' (12 May 1985). In fact only two years earlier—in circumstances which were not markedly different, except perhaps that the government which the Labour Party then supported did not have an overall Dail majority—John Carroll had been equally trenchant on the other side of the argument, issuing a warning that the trade union movement would in certain circumstances break its links with Labour.

'I must also add', he commented ominously on that occasion, 'that we are discussing with the Trade Union Liaison Group of the Labour Party the value of a liaison that is all very much one-sided and would appear to be of little value to trade unions who have been so loyal to the Labour Party ever since its foundation as the political arm of the trade union movement by James Connolly and others in 1912.'

John Carroll's and Billy Attley's strategy is, viewed in the medium term, straightforward enough. They are both genuinely committed to the maintenance of their union's links with Labour, but increasingly worried about the possibility of holding the line against an increasingly restive membership—especially when Labour is in power and when the government of which it forms a part is uttering such heresies as a pay freeze in the public sector. In the Transport Union itself, the closest call came with a threat by that union to ballot all its 150,000 members on the advisability of maintaining the Labour affiliation. It is difficult to work out whether this proposal, which surfaced in late 1984, was part of the traditional sabre-rattling by union executives anxious to impress on the Labour Party that they meant business, or whether it was a tactic that simply got out of control (such a ballot would almost certainly have resulted in disaffiliation), but the proposal was quietly sidelined at the union's 1985 Conference, to the relief not

128

only of the party leader, Dick Spring, but of prominent anti-coalition TD Mervyn Taylor, who spoke of the 'immense damage' to the party that would ensue, were the link to be broken.

The restiveness within each of the two major unions has now, of course, a political as well as an organisational or industrial dimension. This has coincided with, and in some degree is linked to, the growth of the Workers' Party as a political force to the Left of the Labour Party in national politics, and within the trade union movement, particularly (although by no means exclusively) within the ITGWU. It is this added dimension which helps to explain the tension which marks the policy swerves in the John Carroll leadership of that union. Under his predecessor, Michael Mullen, a number of young men began to make their mark in the union, rising more rapidly to positions of influence such as branch secretaryship more rapidly than might have been expected from people of their age group. Most of them did not fit the traditional trade union mould in that, although they might have come from working-class backgrounds, they had third level education and, in a number of cases, a history of prominent involvement with student politics at university and national level. People like Pat Rabbitte and Eamonn Gilmore were national officers of the Union of Students in Ireland before taking up positions in the ITGWU. They have also become prominently identified with the Workers' Party, and both of them have stood for public office as candidates for that party. They and a number of other young Mullen protegés are known somewhat derisively within the Union as 'the students', and are probably feared as much as they are disliked by the more traditional Labour supporters who see them as eroding the old power base. With them has been lumped— perhaps unfairly, because his many attributes do not include a third level qualification—Des Geraghty, another prominent Workers' Party member who has been defeated by the powerful mainstream Labour and anti-Workers' Party (which is not necessarily the same thing) machine in the Union on each of the three occasions on which he has run for important Union offices.

The belief among Labour Party members that Workers' Party support within the trade union movement is more widespread may be correct, or it may simply be a reflection of the fact that it is more visible than it used to be. In the past, Workers' Party activists in the trade union movement tended not to noise abroad their political affiliation from the rooftops. In this, indeed, they were no different from Fianna Fail and Fine Gael trade unionists, but until recently they have found it difficult to shake off the conspiratorial aura which surrounded them in the early days. Latterly, their candidature for public office has brought them very much more into the open. Geraghty, for instance, was the Workers' Party candidate for Dublin in the 1981 Euro-elections, and is a member of the Ard Chomhairle, or executive, of his party.

The sharpness of the needle between Labour and the Workers' Party in the union movement—and especially in the ITGWU—was shown after Geraghty, speaking at his own party's annual conference, criticised Irish trade union leadership in a general way, and suggested that some trade union leaders were to the Right of Fianna Fail on social matters. John Carroll, at his own union's annual conference a few weeks later, made an equally trenchant, and equally non-specific, attack. He had heard it alleged, he said, that 'one or maybe two of our own appointed staff have, it is claimed, on a non-trade union platform called in effect for the sweeping aside of the Irish trade union leadership.'

'If any appointed official', Carroll went on, 'finds it impossible to give the required loyalty to, and support for, the union's agreed policies and elected leadership, well that person can easily resolve such a personal dilemma, as he or she has the absolute personal freedom, as the old saying goes, either to shape up or ship out.'

Carroll's comparison between the 'elected' leadership of the ITGWU and the 'appointed' status of officials like Geraghty could hardly have been more pointed, as was his reference to a 'non-trade union platform'—as if Labour and union leaders had never taken advantage of the substantial platforms provided by Labour Party Conferences. What is sauce for the Labour Party goose may not yet, at any rate, be sauce for the Workers' Party gander.

The official Workers' Party line seems to be not to press for dis-affiliation: it is unlikely that the Union would affiliate to any other party, much less the Workers' Party, and there would be a danger that all Union members running for election, even for Fianna Fail and Fine Gael, would then have a claim to funds raised through the Union's political levy. But their presence—and it is a growing presence—is not calculated to help union leaders sleep soundly at night. Possibly in desperation, the Transport Union Executive decided early in 1985 to cease making its purpose-built conference

130

centre in Liberty Hall available for political meetings—*any* political meetings. One of the first casualties of this was the Workers' Party. In fact, the Labour Party had used it infrequently, for the anomalous reason that they could usually find cheaper accommodation elsewhere. The allegations of Workers' Party 'infiltration' of the unions in general and the ITGWU in particular still, however, surface from time to time in the media, most notably in *The Irish Independent*, which typically published in October 1985 a dramatic story suggesting that two Workers' Party members of the union representation on the Public Services Committee of Congress had played an overtly political role during talks with the government on pay.

If the 1985 Conference decision by the ITGWU caused some surprise in the media—where it was generally interpreted, with some cynicism, as evidence of John Carroll's willingness to support the party leadership in return for other, unspecified favours—it caused something approaching consternation within the group of trade unions affiliated to the party. This is because, prior to that conference, the unions concerned had mutually agreed to support each other's resolutions at conference on the very reasonable grounds that the only chance they had of influencing party policy was to present a united front. The discontent that this created bubbled over subsequently, notably in moves within the ATGWU to suspend its affiliation tot he party until it rejected what it condemned as 'minority participation in conservative coalitions'. The ATGWU district secretary in the Republic (the union is British-based), Matt Merrigan, has been associated with the labour movement for much of his life and indeed, but for one of those splits which appear to be inevitable in that movement, could have become a Labour TD and might still be one today. This was in 1969, after the general election of that year in which one Dublin constituency—Ballyfermot—became the first in the country ever to return two Labour TDs—in this case, Dr John O'Connell and Sean Dunne. Dunne, who refused to abandon or even modify his election campaign despite a worrying medical condition, did not survive polling day long enough even to take his seat in the new Dail. In the run-up to the ensuing by-election the tussle for the nomination was between Dunne's widow, Cora, and Merrigan. When Merrigan succeeded in getting the nomination, a group of people—many of them, it was widely believed at the time, Fianna

131

Fail supporters—supported her candidature as an independent. Even with this disastrous split in the Labour vote, and despite his typically cavalier rejection of Fine Gael transfers in an eve-of-the-poll interview, Merrigan came dramatically close to winning the seat—to within about 300 votes, in fact. His defeat was undoubtedly a tragedy, not only for the Labour presence in that solidly working-class constituency, which became attenuated into a ward machine controlled by Dr John O'Connell, but for Merrigan's own political career.

Small of stature, with a somewhat high-pitched voice, and not given to mincing his words in public, Matt Merrigan has sometimes been vulnerable to media caricature as the kind of trade union leader who makes comfortable middle-class people lie awake in their beds at night. He is also, however, someone who commands a wide respect within the trade union movement for his willingness to mount extremely effective campaigns on behalf of his members and for his relative lack of concern for personal popularity. His subsequent political career, into and out of the Socialist Labour Party, and into a sort of political wilderness as an independent, is yet another example of the kind of fragmentation which has bedevilled the links between the party and its trade union allies. His political activities have now been reduced largely to writing abrasive letters to the newspapers: outside the political mainstream, he pops up occasionally in fringe group activities such as the 'Rainbow Coalition', a loose grouping of trade unionists, unemployed people and residents' and tenants' organisations which was formed during the 1985 local elections to campaign against councillors and candidates who had supported the controversial water charges.

If problems between the Labour Party and the trade union movement are sometimes focused on the tensions between individuals (the much-publicised Budget Day argument in January 1986 between John Carroll and Dick Spring is a case in point), the uneasiness of the relationship is also shown in the nature and amount of the financial contribution made to the party by the affiliated unions. The public perception, outside the party, may be of a political organisation which is largely if not entirely bankrolled by powerful trade unions. One article in *The Irish Times* in 1983, typically, warned of the financial consequences of FWUI disaffiliation from the party because, or so the anonymous writer stated, 'the major unions donate heavily to Head Office funds' (13 December 1985). The reality is quite different. For one thing, corporate affiliation fees are relatively low: in 1981 they were set at £448 for a membership of 4,000, with an additional £72 for each additional 1,000 members in excess of 5,000. Thus the effect of an ATGWU decision to suspend affiliation would mean a loss of some £1,000 to party funds—awkward, but hardly critical, and if anything less serious than the bad publicity which such a move naturally evokes. In 1980, it was determined by annual conference that corporate affiliation fees would be automatically increased every two years in line with increases in the consumer price index. In the hurly-burly of three elections in two years, this provision was lost sight of and when, in 1984, the party's new general secretary, Colm O'Briain, sought to recover the arrears due on foot of this very reasonable decision, his efforts met with stiff resistance and pleas of union poverty, before the inevitable compromise was eventually hammered out.

Between 1970 and 1979, in fact, the trade unions' contribution to party finances actually declined substantially as a percentage of total party income. In 1970, the affiliated unions contributed 27.5 per cent of total party income: by 1979, this had fallen to 15.3 per cent. Between 1974 and 1979, that contribution, in terms of actual cash received, increased by only £300. In 1983, the corporate members (i.e. unions) contributed a grand total of £13,367 to the party's total income of £119,020, representing about 11.2 per cent. That figure, in 1983, was approximately half the total contributed by the party's four MEPs, and covered only a third of the party's expenditure on staff salaries and pensions alone.

The extent—and variation over different time periods—of union help to Labour in financial terms can be readily seen by contrasting figures for one particular union for an election year with those for a non-election year. The FWUI is the second largest union in the country, and, as one would expect from a union founded by Larkin (no matter how controversial the circumstances) has always taken a keen interest in the political fortunes of Labour. In the year 1983–84, the accounts for its political fund for the period up to 31 December 1984, showed affiliation fees to the Labour Party at £1,888, and general election grants for Dail and Seanad amounting to a further £900 (these were presumably grants which had remained unpaid from the previous year. Other bits and pieces brought the grand total up to £43,413, leaving an unspent balance in the fund, which appears to generate about £10,000 a year, of £7,287.

The contrast with the previous year, in which two general elections were held, is striking. In 1982 the Labour Party affiliation fee was the same, but the details tell their own story:

Labour Party Affiliation Fees	£1,888
General Election Grants	4,200
Seanad Election Grants	1,200
Delegate Fees (Party Conference)	120
Delegate Expenses (Party Conference)	2,250
General Election Grant to Labour Party	5,000
Delegate Fees re Coalition Conference	120
Delegate Expenses re Coalition Conference	750
Grant, Dublin West By-election	200
Grant, Galway East By-election	200
El Salvador Trip, Michael D. Higgins	50

The union was enabled to spend so much because—even after the election expenses in the previous year—they still had almost £6,000 left in the political fund. Their total political fund income for the year was in fact £16,510, which gave them a grand total of more than £22,000 to spend. And what goes for the FWUI also obviously is true on a larger scale where the larger union—the ITGWU—is concerned. The annual income to the ITGWU's political fund is of the order of £50,000, making it a very substantial influence—if it chooses to be.

It is easily seen from these figures that the chief clout of the unions operates in election years, and not in the day-to-day running of the party. This can be seen in perspective when it is realised that the annual income of the ITGWU's political fund, just mentioned, is more than twice the total amount of union subscriptions to the party for general administrative expenses each year. Total union affiliation fees in fact account for a much smaller proportion than is the case in Britain. It can be argued that the unions in Ireland have much less power in the party than their counterparts in Britain, but this is not strictly true, either. In 1984–85, for example, a union whose annual affiliation to the party amounted to some £250—the Post Office Workers Union—was able to press some eighty separate amendments to a proposed piece of government legislation by virtue of their association with the party. In other words, they get a lot more for their money than votes at party conference alone might indicate. And even their £22,000 annual total subscription (1985) can be reduced by the £9,000 odd represented by Senator Christy Kirwan's Senate salary, which it is understood goes into his union's funds.

Viewed historically, the financial role of the unions is even more limited today than it has been in the past. In 1970–71, the affiliation fees from the trade unions amounted to about one-third of the party's total income from all sources. Today (1985) that proportion is down to one-sixth. It would be unfair, however, to write off the trade union movement's financial contribution to the party as it appears in the party's central accounts. For one thing, the party occasionally makes special appeals to its affiliated unions for additional finance, and the unions generally respond to these. For another, the bulk of the expenditure from the political funds maintained by such trade unions does not go towards meeting the expenses of the party's central administration, but towards the election expenses of Labour Party candidates who happen to be members of the union concerned. Although trade unions, as already noted, have little direct influence in deciding who shall be nominated in any particular constituency, the availability of union finance for election campaigns—especially for desperately under-financed election campaigns, as tends to be the norm in the Labour Party—can be quite significant. It is not always the case, incidentally, that union contributions to candidates find their way speedily into a particular constituency's election fund: there are instances in which election committees have pleaded with particular unions to ensure that large sums of money which have been sent to the candidate actually find their way into constituency coffers instead of being spent by the candidate as part of his or her personal election effort!

Labour TDs who have achieved status within their trade unions prior to going into the Dail can sometimes hope for union assistance even after they get there. For many years, for example, at a time when most TDs were accustomed to licking their own envelopes and before any system of secretarial help for public representatives had been introduced, Michael O'Leary, as the ranking Dail representative of the ITGWU, had the services of a devoted full-time secretary paid for by that union.

It is in this umbilical link, perhaps, that the main potential influence of the trade union movement on the party as such actually lies. By and large, it tends not to be exercised, and union leaders tend to allow TDs who are members of their organisation to act independently, although they may brief them from time to time on matters of specific importance to the union.

A major exception to this was Michael Mullen, when general secretary of the ITGWU. Quite a number of TDs—including myself—have at one time or another been members of the ITGWU. Within this group, however, there are two sub-groups— those TDs who have been branch officials of the union, appointed to such positions by the executive (in practice, it is widely believed, a form of Mullen patronage), and those TDs who, although members of the union, for one reason or another fall outside the general secretary's immediate sphere of influence.

Mullen himself was a trade union boss of the old school, a sort of Mayor Daley of the Irish industrial scene, who would probably have been at home in a position of power in a major union any- where in the world. Clever and autocratic, he was a powerful organiser who was politically active himself for a considerable time. He was a member of Dublin Corporation and—for a period prior to the 1965 general election—in the position of being the only Labour TD in the whole of Dublin. As such, he occasionally found himself in some astonishing situations, on one occasion being called on to mediate during a hunger-strike being staged by Republican prisoners. His sense of the absurd, he was fond of relating in later years, eventually enabled him to see the ridiculous side of a situation in which one of the key issues to which the confrontation had been reduced—and on which men were apparently willing to starve themselves to death—was whether they should have access to lined or unlined writing paper! He had the trade unionist's attention to detail, but was also given, on occasion, to Pecksniffian pronouncements on matters of universal import. 'The Labour Party', he once said, putting a bumptious interviewer in his place, 'is not a class party . . . Labour does not depend on any particular class for its support; our policies are for the so-called middle class, the working class, and the so-called upper class for that matter—and, of course, the farming community.'

136

He was powerful enough to secure a Labour government nomination to the Senate for the life of the 1973–77 government, and retained it even after losing the whip towards the end of that government's term of office (as did one of his ITGWU successors as a Labour Senate nominee, Christy Kirwan). He not only retained his membership of the party, however, but strained every muscle to secure the election of Michael O'Leary to the leadership after Brendan Corish's resignation.

He confined his efforts at persuasion to those TDs he knew were most vulnerable—those who owed their positions in the union—or thought they did—to his patronage, and who in any case would be slow to offend him. Others were insulated from this kind of approach, notably myself, who—he probably knew well—favoured Cluskey's candidature, and Barry Desmond, who had had the advantage of a lengthy spell working for Congress, and whose links with the ITGWU were of a formal rather than an organic nature.

The less fortunate were pressurised mercilessly into voting for O'Leary, whatever their personal inclinations. Some of them—the late Pat Kerrigan, TD for Cork, for example—found the conflict of loyalties personally distressing to a very high degree. Even thicker-skinned people, such as Liam Kavanagh, found the pressure highly distasteful. Barry Desmond was so immune from the Mullen influence that he actually formally proposed Cluskey as leader at the critical meeting.

A central irony in all this is that, prior to 1969 at any rate, Mullen and Cluskey had been on the same side of the political fence. They had cooperated as members of Dublin Corporation, and respected each other's basic commitment to the trade union movement. After 1969, however, when the conflagration broke out in the North, the two men went in sharply different directions. Mullen's republicanism and Cluskey's fierce anti-Sinn Fein attitude drove a massive wedge between them which was never removed, and from then on Mullen lost little opportunity of criticising the Cluskey leadership. It was not necessarily that O'Leary mirrored Mullen's attitude on the North—in fact he was far closer to Cluskey than to Mullen on this issue. But he served the purpose of providing a focal point for Mullen's relentless opposition.

In July 1983 Dick Spring, addressing the ITGWU annual conference, complained that Labour got 90 per cent of the blame when things went wrong in government, but only 9 per cent of the vote at election time. Later, at a supposedly private, but widely reported, meeting of party activists in Cork, he was less cautious, describing the Irish trade union movement as one of the most conservative in Europe. One recent commentator on the party's links with the unions, Michael Gallagher, has given public expression to the viewpoint that Labour might gain more than it lost were these links, neither umbilical nor life-sustaining, to be totally ruptured. Brendan Halligan has actually suggested that the series of union affiliations to the party in the fifties and sixties did more for the party's image than for its vote, to which it added, he thought, possibly less than half of 1 per cent. But in image terms he underlined the significance of the fact that in 1969 a massive banner was draped across the imposing facade of Liberty Hall in Dublin urging all who saw it to Vote Labour—and the significance of the fact that in 1981 it was not there. The more measured opinion within the party is probably to the effect that, given both the low public opinion of trade unions (not least among trade unionists themselves, who of course always blame members of other unions) on the one hand, and the real disadvantages of disaffiliation on the other, the party has to make the best of a bad job.

The political problems facing the trade union movement, for its part, are not confined to questions of whether or not it should remain affiliated to the Labour Party. The most central one is the degree to which it should become directly involved in the political process, and on this they have blown both hot and cold.

One of the ironies of modern Irish history—and perhaps best understood in this context—is the role played by Sean Lemass in the 1940s, when he introduced legislation to require trade unions to register, and made clear his opinion that there were too many small trade unions in the country. Lemass was not by any stretch of the imagination a socialist, and so his apparent concern for the emergence of a strong and relatively undivided trade union movement must at first sight appear strange. It is more readily understandable, however, if it is considered that Lemass was far-sighted enough to see the political threat from the Labour Party, and in particular from a Labour Party closely linked to the trade union movement. If it is also remembered that the 1930s and 1940s were the heyday of corporatist thinking in Ireland, it is not difficult to imagine that Fianna Fail thinking of that time—and since—envisaged the trade union movement being sucked into direct partnership arrangements with the government of the day, leaving political Labour out in the cold.

Nor was this a phenomenon simply of the 1940s, or of Fianna Fail thinking. There was considerable gratification when the normal wage round negotiations involving the ICTU and the government blossomed into what was called a 'National Understanding', i.e. an agreement between government and trade unions that covered not only the size of the anticipated wage increase for the year ahead, but a whole raft of social welfare and social issues which were the subject of simultaneous government commitments. Some trade union leaders—notably Donal Nevin, present general secretary of the ICTU—are known to have reservations about such a process, precisely because, the more successful it is, the more it makes the Labour Party appear irrelevant, and casts it in the role of some sort of Dail *claque* to applaud the triumphs of organised Labour outside the Oireachtas. On the other hand, any political weakness displayed by Labour in government is likely to promote, among some trade union leaders, the belief that they are better off relying on their own strength than on the allegedly weak reed provided by the Parliamentary Labour Party. John Carroll, for instance, in his presidential address to the ITGWU in 1985, argued that 'the reality is that wages and purchasing power as well as the creation of jobs and the provision of social welfare, health and education services cannot be divorced from the redistribution of wealth and the involvement of the trade union movement in the planning of the utilisation of our national resources and an equitable taxation system'.

The 'corporatist' approach, indeed, while it may have considerable attractions for governments anxious to tie in all possible sources of opposition, and for trade unions anxious to flex their muscles, has for the very same reason considerable constitutional and democratic implications which the trade union movement, no less than the Labour Party itself, would be foolhardy to ignore.

The most recent manifestation of trade union opinion about the appropriate role for Labour in Irish politics came in February 1986, when the group of unions affiliated to the party declared that the party should stay out of government for a decade in order to build itself up as a credible alternative government. In one sense, this particular decision by the unions implied an unwillingness to challenge the existing leadership directly by calling on it to withdraw from the government of which it then formed a part. But its other implications were unmistakeable. Chief among them was the implication that the Labour Party is no longer a credible alternative, at least for trade unionists. The facts, to some degree, support the thesis: during the period when Labour has been in government more often than out of it, wage-earners' incomes have increased at a markedly lower rate than have farmer incomes or corporation profits. And there is the undeniable implication that this is due to a failure of the leadership in coalition. Nonetheless it is surprising, to say the least, that the trade union movement— almost by definition committed to the need for current gains for its membership—should be prepared to settle for the hope of bread in some unspecified future, and to spurn whatever partial gains a smaller party might be expected to make in government.

The other half of the implied bargain is at least as interesting: if Labour takes the advice of the unions, and adopts a voluntary absention from government for a decade, will the unions deliver the votes of their members in return? Can they? And what happens if they don't? A moratorium on coalition would serve at least one useful purpose in this context: it would help to identify which unions are serious about their structural links with the party, and which are not. It would put the gun in particular to the head of the largest union of them all, the ITGWU, whose general secretary, Christy Kirwan, lost the Labour whip in the Seanad for voting against the government early in its term of office, but whose subsequent failure either to resign or to contribute to any significant degree to the workings of that assembly must have given rise to very reasonable Labour feelings that the union was attempting to have its cake and eat it.

It was hardly surprising, in the circumstances, that Dick Spring, within a week, should have combined a swingeing attack on the Progressive Democrats with a ringing defence of the party's right to enter government. A decision to forego coalition looks considerably different to a leadership which has participated in government: it is, effectively, an admission of failure, and this is the most likely—if not the only—reason why it is almost certain to

140

be opposed. Nobody likes admitting that they were wrong, but when the alternatives are to do so, or to be dragged out of government by the unions or by conference, a Labour leader's hesitation is understandable. The problem is that time does not wait on such decisions—and the more unpopular policies Labour becomes committed to in coalition, the longer it will take to re-establish its credibility as a party of policy outside it.

Party Policy: All Cloak and no Dagger?

POLICY is to the Labour Party as opium is to the addict: devotees can never get enough of the stuff. And yet there seems to be, within the party, a permanent policy crisis. It is the purpose of this chapter to analyse the history and the source of this crisis, which may itself be closely related to at least some of the party's electoral problems.

The official fiction is that Labour Party policy is determined by annual conference and so, in a sense, it is. In government or in opposition, the party indulges in policy-making on a scale and with an intensity quite foreign to either of the other two major parties, which regard their annual conferences primarily as vehicles for carefully planned media impact and secondarily as occasions on which rank and file supporters can be allowed to give vent to basically inconsequential sentiments. It was not always thus, and policy-making in the party has gone through several distinct phases. In the early twenties, for example, a considerable amount of thought went into many of the party's policies. Its 1925 education policy document advocated regionalisation—a concept which is just as current (and apparently just as incapable of achievement) today. Up to the 1940s, too, before the disastrous split both within Labour and within the trade union movement which dragged the party back from potentially dramatic electoral successes, policy-making was sinewy and realistic.

The party's deficiencies in the policy area were cruelly exposed by its participation in inter-party governments, particularly the second one, which broke up in some disarray in 1957. There was, at the time, little reflection on the causes or consequences of this policy vacuum, and even as late as the early 1960s the whole business of policy-making was very much a secondary activity. Barry Desmond has observed that during this period many election manifestoes were cobbled together, in an upstairs room above Daniel Morrissey's auctioneer's office in Lower Merrion Street, by himself, Catherine McGuinness, and Donal Nevin.

The flurry of policy-making in the late 1960s changed all that. This culminated in 1969 with the publication of a number of important policy documents. These covered industrial policy (the 1930 concept of a National Development Corporation was revived and filled in), on taxation, social welfare, health, housing, education, agriculture (Tony Brown, the present international secretary of the party and a practising economist, and socioligst Damian Hannan, had a major part to play in this particular document), local government, foreign policy and worker democracy. It was quite a shopping list, by any standards, and would have been added to had the original plan been followed. This envisaged the publication of further, even more detailed policy documents to flesh out the first series—there would have been, for example, an entire policy document on primary education, as part of the exercise of supplementing the original document, which covered education at all levels.

Policy-making did not cease, however. The 1969 documents were soon supplemented by policies on the North (1972), on women (1971), and by a re-statement of the party's general approach, particularly in the economic policy area, which was called 'The Socialist Dimension' and came out in 1980 after a series of conference debates.

Having few policies, in the strict sense of the word, the two larger parties are, in government, relatively unconstrained. With a mass of policy documents—the compilation of party policy produced by Brendan Halligan for the 1981 election weighed as much as several telephone directories—Labour is in an entirely different situation.

At the same time, Labour must have the distinction of being one of the few parties (if not the only one) ever to undertake an election campaign, as it did in 1981, promising the electorate to subject them to a totally new tax. This was the Youth Employment Levy, which I and other candidates advocated earnestly on the doorsteps, and which indeed was eventually introduced. Like many electoral promises—although tragically in this case—it failed to live up to its expectations. This was partly because (a frequent problem with Labour policies) the absence of a fully thought-out strategy for the spending of this money on youth unemployment

143

meant that in its first eighteen months or so, when the public were understandably anxious to see it in operation, much of the money it raised went into the maw of AnCO. The whole idea of a separate fund for youth, which was the most attractive aspect of the idea, never emerged with the same clarity as the visible gap in pay-packets created by the levy itself. Indeed, a closer analysis of the unemployment situation could have shown that whereas youth unemployment was the sexiest political issue of the day, there was —and remains—a proportionately greater need to find resources for the re-training and redeployment of the older unemployed.

The central paradox, however, remains the fact that the party with the most policies is the party with the least prospect of implementing any of them. The mere production of policies, however, is guaranteed to heighten expectations among party members about what will happen if and when Labour achieves any measure of political power. The combination of limitless opportunities for policy-making, heightened expectations, and little or no political power, is, more than anything else, responsible for the Etna-like rumblings in the bowels of the Labour Party which accompany every annual conference and are at their most audible when the question of coalition is being discussed.

Given all this, it is hardly surprising that the present leader, Dick Spring, has tried to quell any tendency to Utopianism on a number of occasions, as for example in March 1985 when he pointedly reminded a Wexford audience, 'Socialism is not populism. It is not the grasping of bogus, easy options. Least of all is the Labour Party's approach to policy to be equated with a desire to deceive the Irish people that there is some magic formula, some miracle answer, which will make existing constraints on policy disappear, and guarantee increased living standards and a sharp and immediate reduction in unemployment.' One of the problems about being a party leader in government in hard times, is that it is easier to tell people what your policy isn't than to implement even part of your vision.

Associated with this permanent problem is the belief—correct enough in its place—that the Labour Party, as a party which aspires to govern the country on its own, must construct policies with this event (however distant) in mind. This belief is a cement which helps to bind the party together, and which gives party activists a special kind of momentum. No matter how remote it may seem, the prospect of eventual single-party government is as much a part of Labour's psychological make-up as it is of anyone else's. The difficulty is that, because of this, the task of elaborating policies which might be implemented by a Labour Party which only has a share of political power—and a fairly small share at that—can be portrayed as selling the pass, and as preparing for the 'inevitability' of coalition.

The result of this is twofold. Firstly, many of the policies which are drawn up are framed in a political vacuum from which all *realpolitik* has been excluded, almost on principle. Secondly, the policies which *are* drawn up for Labour to implement in government are generally devised in negotiations at high speed behind closed doors between Labour and (usually) Fine Gael leaders. They become party policy after six or seven hours of heated and stormy debate at a conference at which roughly a third of the delegates will accept whatever is offered to them, roughly a third will reject whatever is offered to them, and roughly a third has not yet made up its mind what to do.

As an example of the first kind of policy-making, it is difficult to beat the second draft of the 1981 Party Programme already referred to. 'This programme of the Labour Party' it states on the first page, 'is framed to express explicitly the ultimate aims of the Labour Party and to express in unequivocal terms the methods and measures which the Labour Party will adopt when entrusted by the people with the authority of government.' It goes on:-

> As part of a continuous process of creating a free, classless society in which the masses of the people will exercise democratic authority the Labour Party, when entrusted with governmental power, will speedily adopt a fundamental programme of legislation and administrative measures which is outlined here. It seeks as its primary objective to eradicate the exploitation of one class by another, to banish poverty, to promote industry, to stimulate agriculture, to foster commerce, to develop our natural resources, to end violence and to promote the voluntary units of all the people on the island of Ireland.

And it adds:-

> The Labour Party can *only* achieve its objectives by attaining

145

the power of government as the majority party in this country. The present position is a transitory phase on the road to securing the support of the majority of the people.

An earlier reference to the need to carry on a 'day to day struggle to secure immediate improvements in the living conditions of the people' has a somewhat anodyne appearance beside such ringing declarations. The debate between gradualism and all-or-nothing socialism is, in a document like this, something of a walkover for the latter. In practice, the reverse tends to be the case.

The references alone, in this document, amount to ten typewritten pages, covering various policy statements going back to the 1920s. The first draft was even more spectacular, containing no fewer than 418 separate footnote references to earlier policy documents.

As an example of the second kind of policy-making, it would be difficult to better the famous 'Fourteen Points' drawn up by the Labour and Fine Gael party hierarchies—initially by the two general secretaries, Brendan Halligan and William Sanfey—in the run-up to the 1973 election. In its brevity and simplicity, it makes subsequent agreements between the same two parties look like theological documents of extraordinary complexity. It had the additional advantage, of course, that it did not have to be sanctioned by a party conference, as the later ones were.

A 1969 document from the Labour Policy Committee, of which Flor O'Mahony was chairman, pointed to a number of key problems in relation to the party's approach to policy-making. Noting that it was one thing to produce a policy document, and quite another to find the money to pay for the printing and distribution of thousands of copies, the committee said:

> The bulk of the policy documents produced did not serve the purpose for which they were intended. They did not serve as a medium for convincing the electorate of the validity of Labour's approach, because they were not read by the electorate. Equally they did not serve as a means of ensuring a policy-informed party, because . . . the analysis contained in them could not be assimilated by the party membership.

Two deductions can be made from these observations without

146

much difficulty. The first is that Labour is an intensely rationalist party, believing quite passionately that all that is necessary is for the electorate to read its policy documents in order to be convinced of their essential correctness. 'We believe in reason,' party chairman Michael D. Higgins told a meeting of the Labour Electoral Commission in November 1985. 'That is the distinguishing characteristic of the Labour Party. We have attracted people who are interested in reason'.

This endearing and somewhat idealistic view is still at the root of much Labour Party policy-making. Even if it were sustainable, Labour Party activists who advance it almost always overestimate both the physical and intellectual problems of conveying vast quantities of information and argument to an electorate which is perhaps at best indifferent and at worst hostile to any of the party's messages. For one thing, the party has rarely been able to afford to print a sufficient quantity of even its policy documents to get them into the hands of more than a small fraction of the party, let alone of the electorate: the rationalist approach to the whole question of policy formulation has tended to ignore the very practical and vital area of distribution. Fianna Fail and Fine Gael's policy flexibility, as well as their admass approach to politics, have made it possible for them to simplify their policies to the point where policy distribution is most cost-effectively achieved through the medium of large newspaper advertisements containing fewer words than appear on a single page of a Leopardstown race-card.

Secondly, as can be seen from the policy committee's own observations, a major part of the problem was that these policies were not even understood by the bulk of the party members themselves. Overall, the spectacle of a party which prides itself on its policies, and on the appeal of these policies to rational non-members of the party, sending out as its ambassadors people who do not fully understand these policies and who cannot even present them to the electorate in moderate quantities, must continue to be a cause of considerable comfort to rival political groupings. It can of course be argued that the primary function of such policy documents is for internal party education, rather than for mass evangelisation: but the problem of non-comprehension does not go away.

One of the chief recommendations of the 1979 Committee, therefore, was that policy statements should be 'shorter and written

in a more popular style than in the past with a view to wide circula-
tion', and a number of shorter policy statements, directed towards
particular interest groups such as women and young people were
in fact produced in the immediate aftermath of this report.

In fact, and just to complicate matters further, it should be
remembered that there are not one but five different forms of
Labour Party policies. First there are policy documents drafted
under AC guidance and subsequently approved by annual
conference. Secondly there are policy statements adopted and
published by the AC in its own right. Thirdly there are election
manifestoes. Fourthly there are contributions by front bench
spokesmen in parliamentary debate. Finally, according to a
memorandum from the 1979 Policy Committee, there are 'public
comments by leading party members in the form of press
statements or interviews'.

The ever-present possibility, of course, is that policy statements
emanating from these various sources may lack the degree of
consistency which is necessary for reasonable political credibility.
The AC's Policy Committee noted in 1979, with barely concealed
frustration, that 'every effort must be made to ensure that
parliamentary contributions and comments by leading spokesmen
to the media reflect the overall policies adopted by the AC and by
annual conference.' It is not difficult to detect behind this plea a
sense of outrage at—among other things—the thinly-disguised
admiration which Dr John O'Connell, then Labour spokesman on
Health, had been displaying for his government opposite number
in the Dail, Mr Haughey, more especially during the passage of
that Fianna Fail Family Planning Bill, the now notorious 'Irish
solution to an Irish problem'.

If one of the problems about Labour is not that it has too few
policies, but that it has too many, and that it has not yet learned
that analytical essays do not produce votes, perhaps a better way of
looking at the crisis is to take some policy areas in which policy
successes or failures can be looked at dispassionately. In the
economic area, the three major policy areas are undoubtedly
employment, taxation and natural resources (although the last of
these does not attract anything like the controversy that the British

148

Labour Party's 'Clause Four' evokes). In the social area, divorce and contraception are ahead of the field by a mile, followed at a distance by issues like public health policy, children's rights, and— a long way down the field—education. The symbolic area may be taken to include the question of the North, but more important, for our purpose, is the neutrality issue, allied with a number of foreign policy questions on which it may be seen that, to Labour, neutrality does not necessarily mean not taking sides.

The first great battle on natural resources in which Labour became involved in recent years was in 1975 when Justin Keating, as Labour Minister for Industry and Commerce, found himself grappling with the legally and constitutionally complicated issues surrounding the exploitation of the Tara/Bula lead/zinc orebody in County Meath and—less urgently—exploration terms for the companies which, more hopefully then than now, were looking for oil around our coast.

In the case of Tara, he found himself under pressure from a number of different sides. The economic Right, ably led by Fianna Fail's Desmond O'Malley in the Dail, was urging a minimalist approach on the state in the belief that a generous royalty and taxation system would maximise exploitation, employment, and— supposedly—the return of the taxpayer. To Keating's Left were some members of the Labour Party, and Sinn Fein The Workers' Party (as it then was) who were arguing for nationalisation and state exploitation of the resources concerned. An SFWP pamphlet which attracted a lot of attention, and not a few converts, at that time, was published with the catchy title 'What's Mined is Ours', and the SFWP were prominent in an umbrella or 'front' organisation, the Natural Resources Protection Campaign, which included many Labour activists and kept up a relentless barrage of publicity on this and related issues.

Keating's ultimate solution, involving a complicated mix of shareholding and royalty measures, really satisfied nobody, more especially when it emerged that the price paid by the state for its stake in the new Bula enterprise, based on a valuation by a London firm of merchant bankers, Lazards, was about four times higher than anyone had expected. The spectacle of a socialist Minister for Industry and Commerce allegedly diverting several million pounds of public money (tax-free, it was also alleged) into the hands of a number of private individuals in return for a somewhat ethereal prospect of future revenue, was enough to deprive Keating of his socialist credentials in many people's eyes, while his insistence on a continuing role for the state damned him among the free marketeers. It mattered little that he could not have expropriated the resources concerned without a constitutional amendment, even had he wished to, or that the capital and current costs of a smelter for the ore—which his critics saw as another essential part of the operation—were almost literally out of reach. It mattered even less that his oil exploration terms, framed by him and accepted by the oil companies at a time when no oil had yet been discovered, were more advantageous to the state than those operating in many other countries. He had, it was assumed, sold the pass, and the ire of the ordinary voter, after Fianna Fail had cleverly dubbed him the Minister for Rising Prices at a time of tearaway inflation, probably combined with a sense of disillusion felt by the ordinary Labour activist in his own constituency, was more than enough to lose him his seat at the following election.

What Keating was actually about, although never publicly stated at the time, was the creation, in Bula, of a company which would, with state involvement, be the nucleus of an Irish multinational, strong enough to engage the other multinationals on their own terms.

Given an uninterrupted, and strengthened Labour presence in government over the following decade, this strategy, based on a particular view of what was possible for a Labour minister playing a minority part in a coalition government and overseeing a mixed and very open economy, might perhaps have succeeded. The ebullience of Fianna Fail's attack on the vestiges of this Labour plan, when they re-entered government, and unforeseen complications relating to planning permission and geological factors, finally reduced the whole grand design to a shambles. Ten years later, not only had not a shovelful of ore been removed from the Bula orebody, but Dick Spring, as Minister for Energy, Justin Keating's effective successor and leader of the Labour Party, was unsuccessfully attempting to persuade one of the very multi-nationals, whom Keating had opposed, to pick up the mangled remains of Bula and get the mine into production at long last.

It may be that the experience marked Keating in some deep-seated way. Certainly, his horizons shifted after this series of disappointments, and at one time—with the enthusiastic and wildly unrealistic support of Garret FitzGerald—he sought the Coalition Government's nomination to the EEC Commissionership which was eventually allocated to Richard Burke. After some time in the Senate, and a brief spell as a nominated member of the European Parliament, he very nearly pulled off the extraordinarily difficult third seat in the Leinster Euro-constituency, but on this occasion his impressive candidature did not quite carry the conviction that it had in the past.

Justin Keating, as a former member of the Communist Party (a fact about which George Colley taunted him in the Dail) could not have been unaware at any stage of the vital importance of economic policy for any party which described itself as socialist. On numerous occasions—especially after he lost his seat—he referred publicly at Labour Party meetings to the need to get down to the business of policy formulation in this vital area. His name, however, does not really figure on the list of those who worked on economic policy for the party in the years in question: people like O'Mahony, Willie Scally (an economist with the Sugar Company) and Michael D. Higgins were much more involved. Even people without very long memories could find more than a hint of unconscious irony in the fact that Dick Spring, just at the same time as he was assuring the oil companies of forthcoming 'clarification' (i.e. relaxation) of the exploration terms, was putting possibly the final seal on Keating's career by appointing him as chairman of the National Council for Educational Awards. Keating—originally an avowed proponent of the idea that technological education should be brought firmly under the wing of the university system—has had scant sympathy for the role played by this particular institution in the past. Government makes gamekeepers of many former poachers.

In retrospect the Keating strategy, more particularly in relation to oil and gas exploration, can still be seen as something of a high point of Labour influence. This was especially evident in late 1982 when Frank Cluskey, as a minister holding a similar portfolio, fought unavailingly against a Cabinet decision not to take into public ownership the ailing Dublin Gas Company. The decision by the government to pump several hundred million pounds of taxpayers' money into the firm, with very little in the way of effec-

151

tive control or even guarantees, led directly to Cluskey's resignation (although he had not used the resignation threat as a bargaining ploy inside the Cabinet). It also helped to indicate how much Fine Gael, in the intervening years, had firmed up on their own economic policies and their determination to resist Labour initiatives.

A continuing germ of the Labour strategy can still be seen, however, in the genesis and launch of the National Development Corporation, which was described by Flor O'Mahony in October 1985 as designed precisely to set up a series of national enterprises large enough to combat the multinationals. As the 'State Development Corporation' it first appeared in a Labour Party policy statement on industrial development in 1969, when it was envisaged that it would not only establish industries but would 'act as the executive agency for implementing large scale regional development plans'.

Keating had reportedly suggested it—unsuccessfully—to the Cabinet during the 1973–77 Coalition, and in fact it crept into that outgoing government's list of pledges for the future at the time of the 1977 election. This was advanced in evidence by John Kelly during the 1985 Dail debate on the NDC, but without any reference to the decidedly mixed feelings that there had been in Fine Gael about it at that time. It surfaced again, however, as part of the package presented to the electorate in the contest following the fall of the first FitzGerald government, when it was introduced to the press by Michael O'Leary. The then leader of Labour failed, by all accounts, to do the concept justice, contradicting himself a number of times in public and slowly but perceptibly losing what had obviously been a rather tenuous grip on the whole idea.

After the fall of the even shorter-lived Haughey government the NDC surfaced again in the November 1982 joint programme for government as an 'early priority'. It would be three years, almost to the month, before the relevant legislation was introduced in the Dail, and longer again before it was passed. The intervening period had, plainly, seen major Cabinet conflicts about core details of the NDC—another example of the problems created by agreements on policies which are only outline agreements, leaving the crucial details for subsequent negotiation. In these subsequent negotiations the Labour Party, according to a major NDC supporter Mervyn Taylor, won out over Fine Gael, and it was certainly true that in a number of areas the rhetoric, at least, of the

152

Labour Party position had been stitched into the legislation. On some key points, however, it was only possible to hail a Labour Party victory by an extraordinarily optimistic reading of the parliamentary draughtsman's prose and of John Bruton's speeches.

On the question, for example, of whether the NDC would be forced to sell off profitable enterprises with which it was associated or not, the somewhat opaque official phraseology suggested that the NDC would only sell enterprises when it was 'prudent' to do so. Mervyn Taylor's interpretation—'it would be completely imprudent to sell off something that's going very well' (RTE 13 October 1985)—would hardly find much agreement in Fine Gael ranks. It is probably true to say that Taylor's proclamation of victory was designed to nail down a particular interpretation—in the hope that it would eventually be followed—and to rally flagging Labour support for the government, more than an ojective assessment of the legal or industrial future for the Corporation.

The NDC is the main prop of Labour's employment creation strategy, but its proponents have to face a number of thorny problems. The biggest single argument in favour of state-led investment is the now notorious timidity of the private sector in the investment and employment areas—a factor underlined by no less an authority than Padraic White, chairman of the Industrial Development Authority. White, who is totally committed to private enterprise, noted caustically late in 1985 that the country's major private industrial companies had actually made a negative contribution to employment growth in the preceding year, shedding jobs instead of creating them. If the NDC ever manages to avoid the problems of gigantism and institutional inertia, and creates vibrant new industries through public investment in areas such as forestry and mariculture, it will help to give the lie to the all-too-commonly held view that state industries in general are inefficient, overmanned, and a drain on the taxpayer. But its advocates have to contend with the fact that the view just quoted is indeed common, even though it may have its origins in perceived displeasure with one particular state company—CIE— or the depredations of the Revenue Commissioners.

Alan Matthews, a TCD economist who is also a party member, put it succinctly to the Commission on Electoral Strategy in 1985:

The most important fact about state ownership is its deep

unpopularity, even among groups to whom Labour would naturally look for support. The European Value Survey in 1981 showed only 3 per cent of the population favoured state ownership and management of industry, although a significant number supported greater employee participation. It would be wise for the party to recognise that this reaction is not just the result of a media offensive, but reflects in part the frustrations of people, both as workers and consumers, in their dealings with state firms. It is all very well for the party to say that state ownership under Labour would be different, but until we spell out in what ways this will be so there will be a credibility gap.

On the question of employment, the record of the party, as is that of the other two major parties in the past decade or more, has been at best spotty, at worst non-existent. Unemployment has continued to grow at an inexorable rate, regardless of who has been in power, and it would be totally unrealistic to underestimate, in this area, the continuing effect of the dramatic shift of resources away from the developed world (including Ireland) as a result of the exercise of muscle by the oil-producing countries since 1973. The situation is to some extent better in relation to conditions of employment. During the 1973–77 Coalition, it is true, it fell to Michael O'Leary to implement a large number of pieces of legislation in the employment area, such as the Employment Equality Act, the Anti-Discrimination (Pay) Act, and a number of other laws (by far the greatest number passed by any Minister of Labour in a single administration, as it happens.)

The cynics were quick to point out, however, that many of them were passed simply, and perhaps solely, to keep us in line with actual or impending EEC directives (the Act providing for the representation of workers on the boards of state companies could hardly be accused of that, however, nor could the decision to grant an extra public holiday in October each year!). Equally, the ones with major financial implications were the ones whose implementation was longest delayed, and attended by the most controversy.

On employment policy, the party has tended to oscillate between impotence when in government, and generalised condemnation in opposition. Up to the establishment of the National Development Corporation, it could at least argue, perhaps, that its solutions had never been tried, as indeed is hardly surprising when one considers that a pre-condition for the implementation of most of the party's employment policies has consistently been the need for 'the Irish economy to be transformed utterly' (1981 draft manifesto, p. 22). This utter transformation was to involve a high degree of centralisation: indeed, this centralisation was allied, in one major policy document in 1981, with a brave flourish in the direction of a 'fifteen to twenty year plan', which could 'not be allowed to flounder in the face of short term financial problems or the inability of private enterprise to invest'. The continuing goodwill of the electorate during this period was, it appears, to be assumed!

After the National Development Corporation, possibly the most important Labour Party initiative in the economic and financial area was the introduction of the Wealth Tax by the 1973–77 government. This tax operated with effect from April 1975 for a period of three years, during which it probably generated more controversy than income. 'Never', said Finance Minister Richie Ryan when the bill was finally being passed in the Dail after a protracted debate, 'were there so many words said about a measure that will affect so few people.' In fact, fewer than 2,000 people in all were assessed for Wealth Tax, and their total wealth was assessed at £337.7 million. A further 2,196 trusts and non-trading companies indicated that they held wealth amounting to some £172.6 million.

A recent NESC report, however, has shown conclusively that the Wealth Tax structure was so riddled with loopholes, successfully engineered by powerful interest groups, that in practice it was hardly worth the exercise. The aftermath was even worse: when Fianna Fail decided to shelve the tax on their return to power, they manifestly failed to put anything in its place. Given that the Wealth Tax had itself been conceived partly as a replacement for death duties, it followed that the taxation base was being dramatically narrowed at a stroke: nor has it been replaced in the interim. One of the reasons for this is that many Fine Gael TDs ascribed the poor showing of their party in 1977 precisely to the introduction of the Wealth Tax (despite its ineffectiveness) and, as a consequence, a specific wealth tax has been virtually ruled out of subsequent Labour-Fine Gael negotiations. The closest Labour

155

has come, to date, to plugging that particular gap again has been with the introduction of the Residential Property Tax, which raised an even more derisory amount of money and at the same time—because of its very existence—acts as an effective block to the introduction of more effective forms of capital taxation.

The Wealth Tax and Residential Property Tax experience should be sufficient to convince the party of the vital importance, not just of stating principles which should be applied to the development of our taxation system, but of working out capital taxation systems in some detail, whether these are to be implemented as part of a coalition government agreement (in itself a decreasingly likely possibility), campaigned for in the Dail, or simply presented as part of a general election package. The alternative is to continue to insist, in a general sort of way, that all the policies which the party considers are desirable can be financed simply by raking in all the uncollected taxes or by 'making the rich pay for the crisis'. It is undeniable that in Ireland wealthy people, with their access to expensive accountants and the mobility of their assets, can avoid or evade considerable potential taxation, and the tackling of this problem is a political task of considerable urgency. The likelihood is, however, that even though such an exercise—if undertaken with sufficient vigour and even ruthlessness—would undoubtedly improve a government's current revenue figures, its chief value might lie in its demonstration effect. By this is meant the effect that arises when the general body of taxpayers realises that loopholes for the very rich are being progressively eliminated, and is thus reconciled, even to a limited degree, to the continuing need for a level of taxation that is, at least outside the Nordic countries, virtually unique in Europe and especially draconian when compared (as it usually is) to taxation rates in Britain.

The coalition issue will be dealt with in another chapter, but it is important to recognise, in relation to the issues relating to sexual morality, that although Labour has generally—given the foot-dragging of its rural deputies—contributed modestly to the development of these policy areas, its initiatives have not been achieved without difficulty, internal as well as external. When in 1971 the Galway Conference of the party took its decision in favour of contraception, for example (two years after Mary Robinson and I had first broached the question in the Senate) feelings ran so high that delegates actually spat at each other as they left the conference hall. It was hardly surprising, in the circumstances, that the Browne–O'Connell bill to change the law which was subsequently given an airing in the Dail was a private members' bill introduced by these two deputies, rather than one with the full weight of the party behind it.

Four or five years later, although tensions could still arise like summer storms, some of the sting had gone out of these party controversies internally. At one PLP meeting during the 1973–77 government headed by Liam Cosgrave, for example, there was a lengthy discussion on party discipline in the Dail, and the thorny question (then as now) about what to do on 'issues of conscience' arose. Tom Kyne, the Waterford TD who was PLP chairman at the time, had been advocating a fairly strong line on the maintenance of the whip, but paused for a moment to consider other possibilities.

'On the other hand', he said, 'if the government were, for instance, to bring in a bill legalising abortion, I might have to consider my position on that . . . .'

'I must mention that to the Taoiseach,' Conor Cruise O'Brien interposed dryly. 'I believe he has something like that in mind.'

Kyne's intervention was, in fact, crucial at one hotly contested PLP meeting on the question of contraception. As PLP chairman, a non-Dublin deputy—and a former seaman, which was perhaps more relevant—his salty acceptance of the necessity to change the law did a lot at one juncture to quieten the mutterings of opposition which were still to be heard at that stage from the rural baronies.

The other high-profile areas for Labour in the social policy field have undoubtedly been health and education. The wings of its health policies have been decisively clipped, in government, by the shortage of money. Education, however, never ceases to evoke strong feelings at party annual conferences, and is a policy area in which Labour's viewpoint might be expected to appeal particularly to the urban middle-class liberal voter who has been drifting away in the general direction of Garret FitzGerald's Fine Gael. Labour has consistently differed from the other major parties in its insistence on the role of the state, as the paymaster, in the country's educational system. This broadly positive attitude has been underpinned by a fairly strong current of anti-clericalism, of which Noel Browne's statements on clerical control of education are archetypal examples. There are times when emotions become extremely high, as during the tenure of office of Dick Burke as Minister for Education, when the Labour Party Conference in Galway called for his resignation—his fellow-ministers on the conference platform failing signally to come to his defence. His chief offence, in the eyes of party delegates on that occasion, was his willingness to come to terms with religious—and specifically Catholic—demands on the system. Although published Labour Party policy on this issue is clear enough, speeches on this and other occasions betray something of a blind spot, or a concern with the role of one particular church to the exclusion of other religious interests. Once, after a party conference at which I had been sharply critical of the owners of national schools, I was taken to task by a Militant sympathiser for having failed specifically to mention the Catholic Church. I pointed out that the Catholic Church authorities were not the only owners of schools and that, as a non-sectarian party, we could not be expected to single them out. My critic returned to me several weeks later, having thought through his position. He had come to the conclusion, he said, that the Protestant authorities would be perfectly willing to hand over their schools when the time came. In this, as in some other areas, there is a radical soft spot for Irish Protestantism, based partly on its usefulness as a stick with which to beat Catholic obscurantism, and which ignores the fact that—certainly in education—the socially divisive effects of the present denominationally segregated system are no more deplored by Protestants than they are by Catholics. In educational policy, Labour emphasis veers, therefore, between anti-clericalism and the need for more public control—which is at least guaranteed a good show in the media—and attacks on the social effects of the present system, which find less of a welcoming public echo, but which for this reason need to be pursued all the more vigorously.

The debate on Northern policy—a key 'symbolic' area within the party—mirrored, to some extent, the one which was taking place not only in the other political parties (where it was more muted) but within society as a whole, and the struggle to find a policy line

158

which would accommodate the traditional Labour aspiration towards a socialist and united Ireland, a condemnation of violence, and a qualification—however slight—of the Unionists' right to veto all political progress, was not by any means easy. In the process, and given the frightening level of indiscriminate Provisional violence, it was not difficult to see that the aspiration towards a socialist united Ireland became more clearly seen for what it was—an aspiration, not a policy. And, even before the acceptance by conference of the policy document, much of the groundwork for an explicit rejection of IRA fellow-travellers had been done by Cluskey, O'Leary and Desmond. Each of them could exhibit a degree of passion on this topic which contrasted strongly, for those with long memories, with the equal passion with which Labour deputies chained themselves to the Dail benches at one point during the war years to protest against the hanging of a Republican prisoner in Portlaoise. Nor is it possible to under-estimate the effectiveness of the crusade—for it was little short of that—waged against the IRA by Conor Cruise O'Brien. Armed with quite extraordinary verbal dexterity, and an appeal to reason which was none the less effective because it was advanced in circumstances of high emotion, O'Brien could turn heckles, jeers, and the passionate outbursts of Republican party members back at them in such a way that opposition was all but silenced. In this way he could, for example, when invited to condemn illegal violence by the security forces in Northern Ireland, declare in ringing tones that he denounced *all* violence—but more especially the violence that was committed in *our* name. The eventual vote to accept the document took place in an atmosphere that was a combination of drama and farce: O'Brien had wrongly accused Sean Treacy, one of the most hawkishly Republican voices in the party, of failing to support party policy in the Dail on contraception. When Treacy leaped to his feet to deny the charge, O'Brien apologised: the atmosphere, which up to that point had been building up to an almost unbearable intensity, suddenly deflated, and the vote, when it came, was almost an anti-climax.

Some years later O'Brien, speaking at a memorial meeting to celebrate the life and work of one of his oldest friends, Michael McInerney of *The Irish Times*, told a story against himself with which his friends and opponents might both have agreed. After one of Conor's verbal onslaughts on Republicans and Republicanism in print, it appears, Michael—an equally great foe of the Provisionals—had written to him to suggest, with the mildness which was his stock-in-trade, that perhaps there was such a thing as verbal violence, and that Conor might do well to reflect on the legitimacy of this as well.

No such controversies have marked the party's policy on neutrality, in which its assertiveness as against the other two parties has occasionally won it bonus points, notably during the 1977–81 period in the Dail, when Frank Cluskey was not slow to embarrass Fine Gael almost as much as Fianna Fail on the issue when the occasion arose. It is a policy which has a strong emotional ground-swell—so strong, in fact, as to occasionally obscure the fact that the policy is a relatively limited one, and refers primarily to military neutrality, a question which does not generally arise except in the context of any proposal that might be made for a defence agreement between Ireland and NATO, or between Ireland and Britain. Nor was even military neutrality always such a keystone of Labour's position. William Norton, speaking as leader of the party, once gave a very broad hint that a new political arrangement with Britain—and he did not exclude security— might be on the cards in the wake of any successful resolution of the Northern problem. Less frequently examined, also, is the reality that the world of trade is very much a battle-ground, although a non-military one, and that in this context the EEC is as much a limitation on our 'traditional' neutrality as NATO might ever be. Anti-EEC sentiment in Ireland, however, has waned at the same time as pro-neutrality sentiment has grown, and although this contains the seeds of paradox, Labour appears to be relatively well positioned to secure some advantage from the lack of ideological commitment in favour of military neutrality evidenced by substantial groupings within the other major parties.

After 1983, a certain sense of frustration in the policy area led directly to a decision to appoint front bench Labour spokesmen in areas in which the party was not represented in Cabinet: Toddy O'Sullivan, for example, retained a spokesmanship on matters relating to posts, telegraphs and broadcasting, and maintained a fairly high profile during the discussions on the controversial Local Radio Bill. These spokesmanships were utilised only intermittently, and it is probable that their main function was to serve notice on Fine Gael in particular that Labour intended maintaining an independent stance on these issues when—but only when—it suited them.

In government, it is tempting to say, Labour policies have tended in most cases to be defensive ones: policies aimed at protecting ground that has already been gained. And the energy required—apparently—to maintain these defences is such that sallies into open country tend to be few and far between. Two years after taking office, in December 1984, Dick Spring was expressing the policy rationale in terms which clearly expressed a set of priorities. 'In participating in this government we have done so for two (sic) reasons—firstly because we accepted the responsibility following a long and difficult period of instability to restore equilibrium to the process of Government. But there is another key reason—to protect the things we believe in and to progress our policies.' Of the three reasons he actually enumerated, policy implementation came third, and it is not difficult to see why. The second of the three reasons was, in the final analysis, to absorb almost all of the political energy left over after taking care of the first. It could even be argued that if the first reason for taking power in coalition was to restore stability to government, the party was precluded from taking any further action which re-introduced instability.

For most of the period of the government which took office in November 1982 it seemed as if Labour ministers—and in particular the Tanaiste, Dick Spring—had to spend more time chasing Fine Gael hares than sending out Labour Party ones for Fine Gael to chase. This was evident, for example, in the controversy lasting several months in 1984–85 about the size of the projected budget deficit. The Minister for Finance, Mr Dukes, had to be called sharply to account by the Tanaiste on a number of occasions for speeches which would have had the effect—if agreed—of tying Labour in to a politically disastrous series of public expenditure cuts. Again, the long wrangle over the detail of the proposed National Development Corporation, involving public contradiction by Spring of a number of provocative predictions by John Bruton, showed (if you looked at it one way) that Fine Gael were more adept at upping the political *ante* or (if you looked at it another way) that Labour were keeping Fine Gael in their places. Later, a back-bench PLP revolt on the terms of the Radio Bill, led by Frank Cluskey and Toddy O'Sullivan,

161

whereas (he added cheerfully) the Fine Gael Party had been the most successful party of its kind in Europe in resisting wealth taxes and other measures which might erode the economic privileges of its more comfortable supporters. Between July 1983, when the present Coalition Government allocated its first social welfare increase, and the beginning of 1986, social welfare increases amounted to 30 per cent for long-term recipients and 28 per cent for short-term recipients, in a period when the cost of living increase, calculated on a compound basis, had gone up by some 20 per cent. The key political question is whether such increases were funded by those who could most afford to pay, or whether they simply represented a transfer to the poorest from those on middle incomes.

More recently, however, the pendulum seems to have swung back. Whereas the original aim was that policy statements should be directed towards 'specific target groups, selected on the basis that they offered the possibility of optimum electoral gains', the latest series of policy documents appear to have gone back to the older model: those most recently issued, for example, include no fewer than two discussion papers on transport, one on fisheries, one on health, and one on education. The shortest of them is fifteen pages long; the longest is twenty-five; and overall it is difficult to escape the impression that, despite (or perhaps because of) the effort and energy that has been put into them by their authors, they are essentially part of an internal Labour Party dialogue, whose electoral relevance is entirely secondary. This impression is, if anything, reinforced by a statement like the following (from the education document) with which few scientific socialists will disagree, but which would call for more than a bit of exegesis on the average doorstep in the middle of an election campaign.

'Because it is a central mechanism by which class divisions are reproduced from one generation to another, because it is a central institution by which the hegemony of free enterprise ideology is maintained from one generation to another, and because it is being increasingly used to service the workforce requirements of capital rather than the personal requirements of individuals, the education system is a central concern for socialists everywhere.'

As Dick Walsh suggested to his readers in May 1985 (although not *apropos* this particular document), 'For too long socialists and social democratic parties have addressed their constituencies in terms which are clearly incomprehensible . . . the terminology employed in making the socialist case frequently baffles all but the keenest activist.'

Before this problem can be solved, Labour needs to re-examine the basic purpose of its policy-making. Is it to educate the membership, to convince the public, or simply to provide a small group of people with the opportunity to think aloud about better ways in which society could be organised? If these questions can be answered, the policy priorities will become clearer.

8

The Price of Power

AT THE end of December 1985, *The Economist* suggested cheerfully that 'after ten years in eclipse, hopes are brightening for democratic socialists in Western Europe.' Ireland was not to be found among the many examples of this apparent new trend—indeed, it was hardly to be found in the article at all, with only two brief references, one of them in a chart depicting the weakening position of Europe's Communist parties! Is Irish Labour destined to disappear over the horizon, like some political equivalent of Halley's comet, to reappear only at very long intervals? Or is it set on an irreversible journey towards some black hole into which it will ultimately disappear, its component parts spinning off into Fine Gael on the Right and the Workers' Party on the Left? The prediction that this will happen comes equally from those who are afraid that it will, and those who hope that it will: but the evidence is of decline, not of dissolution. And the Labour Party has declined, in different historical circumstances, to an even lower level—to eight Dail seats, in fact. Punchdrunk and bloody, it has staggered back off the electoral ropes again and again, and commonsense would suggest that it can continue to do this for quite some time, perhaps even indefinitely. But the real question is whether this cycle of decline and recovery, always on a small electoral base, is politically inescapable, or whether it is within the power of the party to make a quantum leap which will introduce a new kind of politics to Ireland.

It is essential, therefore, to look at the reasons which are generally advanced for Labour's inability to break the mould of Irish politics in the past, in order to have a clearer view of the options it faces in the future.

It is sometimes suggested that Ireland is too unconventional to be counted among the family of European political systems. This is an analysis which is often offered more vocally by local apologists as an explanation for Labour's failure ever to be more than half a party in a two-and-a-half party system. Analysts inside and outside Labour attempt to explain (if not always to excuse) its failures not only on the grounds that it has participated in a number of unpopular coalitions, but also in terms of the particular historical circumstances with which it has had to contend. These are usually enumerated as the absence of a strong industrial working-class base, the all-pervasive influence of political nationalism and the strength of organised religion.

Peter Mair speaking at the UK Political Studies Association Annual Conference, in April 1985 is one analyst who took the first two of these theories at face value, and he has convincingly argued that, while the factors mentioned are important, they cannot be held wholly responsible for Labour's lack-lustre electoral performance, and certainly cannot explain it away. To blame Labour's failure on the lack of a large industrial working class, he points out, is to conveniently ignore the fact that Labour has never done well even in those areas in which such a class did exist: even in June 1927, when it succeeded in electing twenty-two TDs, only three of them were in Dublin constituencies. Equally, the growth in urbanisation and the flight from the land between the late 1940s and the early 1980s failed totally to provide Labour with anything like commensurate gains. On the nationalist question Mair, while acknowledging the seriousness of the situation created by Labour's decision to abstain in the general election of 1918, argues forcefully that it was not necessarily terminal. To accept this would be to throw in the towel and blame an event that took place more than sixty years ago and this, he suggests, is to accept a level of political powerlessness which would negate all political activity.

The strength of organised religion has undoubtedly been a factor. The Catholic Church has frequently paid more attention to the supposed threat posed by socialism than appeared to be warranted in the circumstances. 'Particular care should be paid to the working class', it thundered on one occasion, 'lest, lured by the promises and deceived by the frauds of socialists, it loses its ancestral faith' This kind of anathema was not uncommon in pre-Conciliar Ireland. But it hardly explains by itself the fact that in other European countries, equally clericalist in background,

165

religion has not been such a brake on the development of organised socialism. If religion has been a factor, it was in alliance with other factors, such as under-development, isolation, and emigration. The problem about most Irish Labour voters, it could be argued, is that they were voting Labour in London, Glasgow, Manchester, Birmingham and Liverpool. And the ancient hostility of Irish catholicism to socialism has to some degree been called in question by the emergence of a more radical clergy, who with many committed lay Catholics have evolved a rationale for the argument that socialism and catholicism are not necessarily mutually exclusive.

Faced with a past that does not offer much hope, and a future that appears to offer even less, what is the Labour Party to do? The first requirement is that it should take its decisions with the minimum of navel-gazing, and with maximum appreciation of the fact that it operates in a fundamentally hostile environment. It should also recognise that a critical element in that environment is the electoral system iself. In fact, Labour strategists in the past may have spent too much time analysing the social and economic structures in society, and too little looking at the political structures within which Irish socialists are trying to carve out a future for their ideas. They will complain—as Michael D. Higgins does with verve and indignation—about the excesses of the 'clientelist' system, in which service delivery rather than the classic Left–Right divide becomes the hallmark of representative politics. Everyone hates it, but nobody knows how to challenge it. They should now examine the question of whether a change in the electoral system is not essential if the unacceptable elements of clientelism are to be attacked, and whether such a change would be to Labour's advantage. Independently of any possible change in this area, they should also map out urgent priorities in the areas of policy, organisation, and strategy. These should allow the party to get down to the job of winning votes and seats without either allowing internal dissension to tear it apart, or retreating into an idealised and self-satisfied opposition stance in which all the options are soft ones.

An essential part of this argument about the electoral system is that the party, which was an initial beneficiary of PR and which fought strenuously to retain it—notably with its famous slogan for the 1966 referendum (coined by Brendan Halligan) 'The straight vote is crooked—vote NO!'—is a long-term loser from the system, and that it should be seriously considering alternatives.

Developments outside the electoral system have encouraged a political emphasis on service delivery, and the blurring of ideological distinctions between parties as individual politicians try to outdo each other in delivering services (houses, social welfare benefits, jobs, etc). It is also inescapable that the Irish electoral system magnifies these tendencies to a dramatic extent. In the multi-member constituencies, the theory is that each TD has to look after, on average, between a third and a fifth of the total electorate. It is true that to some extent active supporters of a particular political party will, when they need help or advice, turn first to the TD from their own party. But there are always people without a TD and, more importantly, people who feel that they have an equal right of access to all TDs, irrespective of party, and that a TD's effectiveness as a public representative can be measured solely by the criterion of service delivery.

This has several effects. In the first place, it produces a type of constituency commitment and workload for the average Irish TD which would make a British MP turn pale. If the British complaint is that the MP is too remote from his constituents, the Irish equivalent is that it seems to be impossible to get a TD to turn up in the Dail. Secondly, the actual parliamentary work tends to be left to front-bench spokesmen, to political neophytes, and to elder statesmen doing a lap of honour before graceful retirement. Tim McAuliffe, a Labour Senator for many years, was once heard to remark during a rowdy PLP meeting when one of the protagonists departed in a hurry to make a speech in the Dail chamber, 'There's more people lost their seats in here by opening their mouths up there than some of you realise!'

More corrosively, of course, the system encourages constituents in the belief that political intervention will get them benefits to which they are not entitled (as it occasionally does) and, no less importantly, encourages hard-pressed or devious politicians to find ways through, around or behind the system to reward particular clients. The fact that much of this constituency work may be unnecessary, irrelevant, or even a perversion of the course of justice is of course quite beside the point. As long as there is one TD who is prepared to write an unnecessary letter, all of his or her colleagues will feel obliged to follow suit in the belief that their

167

failure to do so will tell against them at the polls. One of the few TDs ever to stand out against this practice—and, with his name, he was probably the only one who could afford to—was the late Vivion de Valera, who used to reply to housing applicants with a standard letter to the effect that their application was governed solely by local authority regulations, and that if they were entitled to a house they would get one, otherwise they would not.

Given that in most Irish constituencies the Labour Party organisation is the smallest and the weakest, it follows that it must suffer most from a system which rewards, or is thought to reward, service delivery above all other political functions. By trying to match the performance of the larger parties, and (inevitably) failing, it actually helps principally to draw attention to their success. The service delivery objective in politics, to put it another way, is one which inherently favours the larger parties, and which is itself enhanced by multi-member constituencies in which representatives are elected by the single transferable vote.

There is, of course, nothing wrong with service delivery in principle and there would be something strange about any form of politics which precluded it. Many Labour public representatives are individually good at it, particularly on behalf of the under-privileged. This is the case across the Labour spectrum, and there is little truth in the occasional supposition that it is the 'intellectuals' in the party who do not do this kind of work because it causes them ideological problems. The constituency work of Labour people like Michael D. Higgins, or Mervyn Taylor, is a clear indication that there is no necessary link between left-wing opinions and a dismissive attitude towards one's constituents. Within the Irish political system as it exists at the moment, however, it tends to make Labour even more of a marginal party by making it fight battles on ground chosen by its larger and better organised opponents.

But there is another aspect of the present PR system which may be said to militate against the emergence of ideological politics, and hence against Labour, in an even more fundamental way. This is the observable fact that on issues which do have a strong ideological content, the existence of multi-member constituencies —particularly of such constituencies which are small by European standards—tends to drive all public representatives into the centre of the ideological spectrum. In closely-contested three-seat constituencies, for example, the transfer of a few hundred stray votes relatively late in the count can make all the difference to winning and losing the last seat. Aspirant or sitting TDs of all parties are therefore concerned, insofar as it is politically possible, to minimise the ideological differences between themselves and at least some of their opponents. This will be true even in the larger, five-seat constituencies, where the tendency for votes to transfer within the same geographical area, rather than on grounds of ideological compatibility, can be quite marked. This has been most obvious in questions such as those relating to contraception and divorce, where the pace of Dail progress towards change is only outwardly determined by the attitude of whole political parties and of their TDs. More fundamentally, a TD's attitude on issues like these is determined less by his party's policy, no matter how well-established, than by the likely attitude of the other TDs who share his or her constituency. The pace of social change in each constituency, therefore, is largely determined by the pace of change of the most conservative TD. This can have quite dramatic results on political behaviour at parliamentary party meetings, and at elections.

Labour could be better served by another system, such as the single-seat constituency elected by the transferable vote. A version of this system operates in Australia where, despite considerable attempts at gerrymandering by the Liberals, it has not prevented Labour administrations from taking office. And it has been used for elections in Ireland in the past, although not in the Republic. It was used for the single-seat university constituencies of London, Wales and Belfast, before the abolition of university representation at Westminster in 1950. Indeed, in the case of Queen's University, Belfast, it produced in Sheelagh Murnaghan one of the few unpredictable, honest and courageous voices to emerge from that political system during that entire period.

Such a system, while not offering the full advantages of a PR system such as we have at the moment, would undoubtedly minimise some of its disadvantages without veering towards the inherent unfairness of the British system. It would require any candidate to receive a minimum of 50 per cent of the vote before being elected, and so would undoubtedly lay as much importance on transfers as does the present system. By reducing the number of TDs per constituency to one, however, it would sharply reduce the electoral blackmail which is visited on many present TDs by local pressure groups and by his or her peers, and leave the TD with more time in conscience to attend to Dail duties.

From Labour's point of view, however, there is an additional advantage which would not—like the ones I have enumerated—accrue also to the larger parties. These parties are fundamentally catch-all, centrist parties. In order to appeal to all sections of the electorate, they generally operate by choosing a slate of candidates which mirrors the social composition of each particular constituency. In Dublin South, for instance, Fianna Fail chose as candidates the 'working class' candidate Niall Andrews, and the 'middle class' candidate Seamus Brennan, and succeeded in getting both elected. Fine Gael, in a constituency in which its support was more definably middle-class, had the opportunity of choosing a working-class candidate—Councillor Tom Hand—whose function was not to get elected but to sweep up working-class votes that might otherwise have gone to Labour, and transfer them up the line to the ultimately successful middle-class candidates.

It is impossible to blame political parties for acting in such a manner, when the electoral system encourages them to do so. But is it not time that Labour, in particular, looked with a clear eye at this phenomenon and began to discuss other possibilities? The single-seat option would at the very least make it more difficult for the larger parties to put up candidates representing opposing class interests under the same party banner. It would not prevent working-class Fine Gael or Fianna Fail candidates being elected in working-class constituencies. But, if it ensured the election to each of the larger parties of TDs who represented ideologically more coherent electorates, it would at the very least force the inherent contradictions in some of these parties closer to the surface. And it might also have the positive effect of creating, perhaps for the first time, a network of safe, or relatively safe, Labour seats which could be used as the launching platform for a Labour assault on other constituencies.

The obstacles to any such a change are not negligible. TDs who felt that their seats were the ones threatened by any change would be among the first to object. There might well be objections also from members of the public alarmed at the prospect of a change that would deprive them of their traditional ability to have each-way political bets—insisting that their politicians appear on the doorsteps at frequent intervals to nursemaid their most minor grievances, while complaining at the same time that they never turn up in the Dail. But there is also a case to be made for the argument that this is not the only possibly beneficial constitutional change, and that Labour policy on constitutional change—which has up to now been confined to calling for a new constitution, or for deletion of the section on divorce—should explore some totally new options. These could include the possible introduction of a list system, or the introduction of fixed-term parliaments. The former might reduce the power of the rural fiefdoms, in Labour and in the other parties. The latter might add to internal tensions in the larger parties by removing some of the pressure traditionally exercisable by party whips. Either way, Labour has little to lose by exploring this policy area and starting a national debate on ways in which the character of Irish politics is shaped by the system we have been living with for half a century.

Whether this type of change is on the agenda or not, the remaining questions of policy, organisation and strategy need to be addressed with clarity and conviction.

The greatest temptation facing Labour at the moment is to attempt to re-create the golden days of 1969 in the belief that the party can be put back on the track from which, or so it is argued, it was abruptly de-railed. This approach runs the very real risk of attempting to drag the party and its policies back to an Ireland that no longer exists, and perhaps did not exist even then. It also risks imprisoning the party in a rhetoric which is internally satisfying but which does nothing for the party's electoral appeal and which is in any case a grossly inadequate way of describing present-day political realities.

Part of the mythology of 1969 is that there exists a 'working class' which is ready for the taking by the Labour Party, if only it renounces coalition. This conveniently ducks any hard-nosed analysis of what precisely the working class is, and of why it does not vote for Labour in any great numbers at the moment.

The easiest definition of the 'working class' is that it comprises all those who are employees. Here, indeed, there would seem to be grounds for hope: three quarters of the working population are

171

now included in this category. At this point the language of politics itself begins to cause problems, because it is evident that not only do many employees stubbornly refuse to consider themselves as 'working class', but the same would be true even of the many semi-skilled and skilled manual employees who form the great bulk of Labour (and Workers' Party) voters. In effect, there is an unresolved conflict between two definitions of 'working class'—the definition I have mentioned, and the 'horny-handed sons of toil' definition, which would restrict the description, by and large, to unskilled, semi-skilled and skilled manual workers, organised in trade unions and possessing industrial as well as political muscle. The latter definition is favoured by the more romantic type of Labour supporter, as well as by the Militant Tendency, which enunciates its policies from within what Ken Livingstone has called a 'workerist *laager*'.

There are a number of political problems with either definition. For example, even though the bulk of Labour and Workers' Party support comes from among the working class defined in such traditional terms, the proportional working-class vote of both these parties *combined* comes to less than that received by Fine Gael and substantially less than that received by Fianna Fail. Even if Labour were to capture 100 per cent of this 'traditional' working-class vote, it would still probably end up with less than 30 per cent of the seats in the Dail—a substantial advance on its present position, it is true, but dismayingly far from the overall majority which is presumed by many of the party's policies. It is also significant that the pattern of trade union affiliation to the party has not followed the evolution of the trade union movement itself. Specifically, the affiliated unions are the more traditional ones. The newer, white-collar unions which represent a growing number of employees, remain outside the fold.

The 'workerist' approach was not popular even in the heady days of 1969. The canvasser's handbook for that election, posing the question, 'Isn't the Labour Party a "one-class" party, which appeals only to a narrow section of our community?', answered forthrightly:

> This is completely untrue. One need only look at the National Panel of Labour candidates to see that the Labour Party is now a national party, appealing to and drawing

support from all sections of the community. Among our candidates are farmers, industrial workers, solicitors, university lecturers, businessmen, professors, housewives, shopkeepers and teachers, in fact members of every section of society in Ireland today.

One obviously significant point is the omission from this list of the occupations of a number of people who were not only on the 'National Panel' of candidates, but who actually succeeded in being elected: publican (Michael Pat Murphy), bookmaker (Stevie Coughlan), trade union official (take your pick), CIE employee (John Ryan), or even shopkeeper (Joe Bermingham). Even more significant is the inclusion, as three *separate* categories, of 'university lecturers', 'professors' and 'teachers'. This provides dramatic evidence, if such was needed, that the Labour Party was at that stage moving rapidly *away* from traditional definitions of its preferred electorate, and following the evolution of society. But these traditional definitions still hold powerful sway among some sections of the party. A failure to challenge them may in the long run do more harm than good, especially when the end result is a ringing appeal to large sections of the electorate to turn the clock back by accepting a description of themselves as members of a class from which they believe they have escaped.

There now appears to be a majority of the electorate who consider themselves to be middle-class, however the sociologists or the ideologues may describe them. If this is the case, then there is no future in Ireland for a classic working class party, because there is no social basis for it. This view is underpinned by trends in employment and technology, which set major questionmarks against both the concept of full employment, and the nature of work in the future. Ferenka and Mostek, among many others, are potent signs that the mammoth single-site enterprise is the enterprise of the past, not of the future, and that the growth of service industries and computerisation will divide and sub-divide work units, down to and including a substantial extension of home-based employment. This will pose major problems for a Labour Party whose concept of industrial development is rooted either in notions of Victorian magnificence (whether owned or managed by public bodies is almost beside the point) or even in 1970s ideas of the gleaming, but still sprawling, chemical or electronic emporia. It will pose even bigger problems for the unions, and it is perhaps not surprising that a number of European unions are rapidly abandoning the battle to maintain such workplaces, and the work patterns which went with them.

A related problem for the traditional Left, in rhetoric as well as in policy terms, is the financing of the public expenditure programmes which have always been part of its political programmes. Socialist models for public expenditure are commonly supposed to depend on policies producing a heavy yield from capital taxation. This is not so. European socialist parties have in the past relied far more on economic buoyancy, rather than on swingeing taxation, to finance their social and industrial programmes. And most of them, in addition, pre-date the oil price shocks of the middle 1970s. The simultaneous reduction in the amount of money available, especially for social programmes, may hit Ireland specially hard, given that the demands on our social services, particularly by the old and the unemployed, may well increase. This is a vital point in a society like Ireland where about one third of the population now receives social welfare payments. This compares with one-fifth in the 1960s. When this figure is added to the figure for those wage-earners directly or indirectly employed by the state, the dominant position of the state in the existing economy can be seen very clearly indeed. However, state payments, especially to those on welfare, are funded out of general taxation to a much higher degree than is the case elsewhere. One EEC survey in 1985, which merited no more than the briefest of mentions in the media, pinpointed the extraordinary fact that within the EEC, on average, 30 per cent of social protection spending (unemployment, sickness, health, family income supplements, rent and mortgage subsidies and pensions) came from the state. In Ireland, on the other hand, the proportion was more than double this figure at 65.6 per cent. The figure for the other nine EEC countries (as they were then, before the accession of Portugal and Spain) was undoubtedly even lower than 30 per cent. In other words, private sector contributions to social welfare in Ireland are about half of what would be expected in any other EEC country—which does not, of course, prevent the private sector from complaining mightily about the present level of such contributions, or about the need to provide a favourable climate for investment, despite the fact that

174

Ireland has the lowest capital taxes, and some of the lowest corporate profit taxes, in Europe.

————————

The policy challenge facing Labour in these circumstances is to go back to first principles. In economic terms, this must mean remembering that traditional Labour strategies are not ends in themselves, but means towards an end. Part of the difficulty is that, in a country which has seen so little full-blooded socialism in practice, the means do become the end, and certain myths—that nationalisation, for example, is always and everywhere a good thing—become almost overpowering.

Labour should now look at some of its most cherished sacred cows in the light of the degree to which—if at all—they contribute to what should be the two key objectives of a socialist society: economic efficiency and distributive justice. It should also decide which policies need to be highlighted as having a definite appeal to the electorate, and which it can afford to put on the back burner.

In the economic area, the Labour Party policy on the need for state-led investment in profitable enterprise is now as fully worked out as it is likely to be, and little electoral gain, in or out of government, may be expected from any attempt to refine it further. As a job-creating strategy on its own, however, it simply lacks public credibility, and needs to be supplemented by other policies. There is plainly a need, for example, for a re-shaped policy on worker participation in the control and management of enterprise. At the very least, the 1969 draft policy document in this area should be taken down from the shelf and dusted off.

As a policy, it has the considerable merit—from Labour's point of view—that it will be viewed with suspicion or even outright hostility by the other major parties. At the same time, it has considerable electoral potential, unlike the party's National Development Corporation, which can be made to appear as yet another white elephant by politicians and media who are opposed to its objectives. And Labour must also learn to look positively at the employment potential of *small* businesses owned by the people who work in them, not just because these offer considerable hope for the future, but because it will help to offset the party's heavily statist image with the electorate. Finally in this area, it must

175

confront the problems posed—and the opportunities created—by technology. Technology can be used to make a decreasing pool of (mostly) male workers considerably richer, at the cost of an expanding number of unemployed, or it can be used to create new freedoms for all workers. If Labour does not take these challenges on board, the critical decisions about technology will continue to be made by the employers.

Where taxation is concerned, Labour must—taking the NESC report on the Wealth Tax as its starting point—identify those parts of the system where the wealthy are evading tax to a massive degree, and frame detailed policies to stop these loopholes. It should not pretend that such action will cure the country's fiscal problems at a stroke, because it will not. But if justice is to be seen to be done, such policies are not only financially but politically essential. It must challenge the received wisdom that the full range of the tax incentives currently available to private industry is essential. It must also force the electorate to look again at the £500 million a year given to both industry and agriculture in direct grants, many of them of dubious value. Above all, it must resist the temptation to take the present economic structure as immutable. Too much of Labour's energy in the past has been directed towards devising new mechanisms to stick on to the existing superstructure, rather than looking at the way in which the system works and applying radical surgery where necessary.

In the social sphere, the aim must be to reconstruct (if indeed it ever really existed) the coalition between potential Labour supporters who see socialism in terms of state intervention in the economy and those who see it as the source of vital initiatives aimed at equality and personal freedoms. Part of Labour's difficulty is that its central coalition is not the classic European pattern of an alliance between working-class radicals and middle-class liberals, but between the former and rural conservatives. Nor are all middle-class liberals the fickle, trendy characters that some Labour strategists believe. A clear line can be drawn between those whose interest in liberal issues stops short at anything which might actually threaten their own life-style, and those whose concern for greater equality is at least as pronounced as their concern for personal freedoms. Thus, the large group of people who favour the introduction of divorce will include liberals from both camps. This is not a reason why Labour should shun the issue. On the contrary, it should make the most of its differences from the other parties where divorce is concerned, and it is difficult to see how it can lose by doing so. It may well be that its failure to be forthright enough about this in the past—although the present leader, Dick Spring, has gone further on this issue than any other leader to date—may be in part responsible for the extraordinary phenomenon that the graphs for divorce reform and for Labour Party electoral support have for some time been moving in opposite directions—the first up, the second down. Issues such as creating a genuinely democratic educational system, or a health system which would make the wealthy pay for unsubsidised health care if they choose private medicine, will separate those who believe in equality from those who are interested in social change only as long as it does not cost anything. People for whom belief in equality is the dominant political motivation are a large and valuable constituency, and if Labour neglects them in order to preach a hoary rhetoric, conceived in the middle of the industrial revolution a century or more ago, it will deserve to lose them.

It is important to buttress, as Labour has to some extent succeeded in doing, the living standards of the poorest in our society. But across whole areas of the country's health and education systems inequality is not accidental but deeply structured into the system. In each of these areas, there is a privileged minority and an under-privileged majority—fertile ground, one would think, for Labour policies. There is also massive, anti-social subsidisation by taxpayers in general of a well-off elite. It should be Labour's priority to identify these elites, and the mechanisms by which they are subsidised, in terms which will allow the electorate to see the nature of the confidence trick that is being perpetrated on them. There is already some evidence that criticism of powerful medical elites, for example, is electorally popular: there seems to be no reason why the same should not be true of educational elites. The under-expenditure on primary education, in particular, and the huge public subsidies to second-level schools that are allowed to operate like independent republics when it comes to selecting their pupils, are two of the most powerful ways in which privilege is written into the system. Actual or potential Labour voters do not, on the whole, have time to study lengthy treatises on these issues—but they will respond to campaigns against them that are clear, consistent and provocative.

177

These and other campaigns can only be launched by an organisation which has done more than Labour has to date to rid itself of its essentially amateur approach. In the late 1960s, the advent of Brendan Halligan and other newcomers did an enormous amount to re-shape the way in which the party was going, but Halligan's opting for electoral politics left something of a vacuum which was only decisively filled with the appointment of Colm O'Briain. O'Briain's tenure of office may have been too short to effect lasting change: the party may have been shaken, not stirred. But some of the steps that need to be taken are at least clear, even if it is uncertain whether or not they will be. For a start, the party needs to take out of its constitution matters that are essentially the subject of regulations, such as branch sizes, financial contributions and so on. Leaving them where they are makes changing the party's internal dynamic, or raising the substantial amounts of money which a modern political party requires, as difficult as turning a double-decker bus in a school playground. Labour should also look again at the underlying structure of its own constitution, which gives a major role to branches, and marginates constituency organisations. Constituency organisations, after all, are the ones which win—or fail to win—Dail seats. And in terms of annual conference, it should critically examine a system which allows a constituency like Dublin West, one of Labour's disaster areas in the capital, to send more voting delegates to the party's supreme decision-making assembly than its neighbour, Dublin South-West, which returns one of Labour's best TDs, Mervyn Taylor, to the Dail. There may well be a case for arguing that while every constituency should be represented at annual conference, there should be a premium for constituencies which succeed in attracting their electorates to support Labour candidates. In that way, too, conference might become more representative of those who actually vote for the party, which presumably is the intention in any case.

All this, of course, begs one of the most central questions of all: can a party with the kind of policies outlined above operate successfully in government today? It is a question that has not really been answered up to now, because—with the possible exception of the NDC—Labour has never put any of its structural policies to the test by making them a condition of government (its influence on education, for example, has always been marginal). If it had done so, it might have succeeded—or there might have been a fresh general election. What has actually happened is that the party, given the choice, has preferred to concentrate on the policy objective of 'carrying on (the) day to day struggle to secure immediate improvements in the living conditions of the people' (Party Programme, 1952, p.2).

The central argument of the anti-coalition group is that there is a fundamental incompatibility between participation in government, at least as a minority partner, and the implementation of any Labour policies worth talking about. Allied to this is the inescapable fact that since the 1940s, given the opportunity to be part of a governmental alternative to Fianna Fail, Labour has never once refused. And, after joining another party or parties in such a government, it has never withdrawn or brought down such a government on a point of Labour principle. Up to 1973, this could easily have been regarded as a piece of history, and a piece, moreover, that the builders of the new socialism could readily discard. In the twelve years since then, however, this apparently historical strategy has been iron-bound, ensuring that Labour has shared power for two thirds of the time, despite a declining vote and increasing internal dissension about the wisdom of its strategy. Some of its influence has been undeniable, but it has also paid a price in that it is being seen increasingly as part of the establishment at a time when parties as disparate as Sinn Fein and the Progressive Democrats—not to mention the Workers' Party— are harvesting a growing public disillusion with politicians and even the system as a whole.

The diminishing size of the PLP has actually contributed to its propensity to enter coalition. This is because, the smaller the PLP, the greater the proportion of its members who will hold office in a coalition government. Of Dail deputies in the present PLP, half hold office of one kind or another, so that even in the unlikely event of their being a split between the office-holders and the non-office holders, the rebels could hope for nothing better than a tied vote. The nature of the PLP is such as to make this a distinctly unlikely possibility. As the party's Dail representation has diminished, however, the concern among party activists about their role in government has grown, and the Killarney strategy, as a result, has come under severe strain. Even if it is re-affirmed, the problem will not go away, but will simply re-surface in a more intense form in three years time. If rejected, the danger is that the party will simply go back in time to 1957, when it adopted anti-coalitionism as a reaction to its unsatifactory performance in government, and was never confronted with any other questions, or any other options.

The coalition gun is a powerful weapon, but it can only be fired once in a while, and this markedly limits its value. One of the problems it creates, for example, is that for as long as it exists as the central strategic question in the party, it obscures the development of genuine Left–Right arguments. Labour activists who are opposed to the leadership for all kinds of reasons will readily grasp anti-coalitionism as their banner, no matter how conservative they may be on other issues. And the equation of 'Left' with 'anti-coalition', while it simplifies the newspaper commentators' jobs enormously, stereotypes the party in such a way as to ensure that its policies and its personalities rarely get a satisfactory hearing. But if the party itself is confused about who belongs on the Left and who on the Right, how can it expect to educate the public in these matters?

Labour Party activists and the Labour leadership need to work out the answers to a number of key questions before the coalition problem can be satisfactorily resolved. As it is, there are some people within the party who are quite happy to see it play a minor brokerage role in Irish politics for the indefinite future. This is obviously a hopeless position, conservative and 'practical' in the worst sense. People like these don't ask questions, they just count votes. But if Labour is to grow, certain questions have to be posed and answered, and it is a basic strategic failure on Labour's part that it has not directly faced them to date.

The central question, which comes before arguments about how Labour should exercise the balance of power, is whether it actually wants to achieve the balance of power or believes in a long-term strategy which would cast it in a role of permanent opposition in the Dail until the electorate turned to socialism in the required numbers. This is what some members of the party may mean by 'socialist opposition', although that phrase has never been satisfactorily enough fleshed out to allow one to know what precisely it means. If, on the other hand, 'socialist opposition' includes the option of abstaining in the Dail on occasion, whether in the vote for a Taoiseach or in votes for social and economic measures, then it is not 'opposition' in this sense, but a variant on the policy of supporting a minority government. This is because minority governments can be supported as much by abstentions as by votes in favour, especially when they are minority governments formed by the largest single party in the Dail.

If, as seems likely, hard-line socialist opposition is a minority opinion within the party, the two other options available are confined to coalition, and support for a minority government. But before the wisdom of one or the other course of action can be explored, a number of tactical questions need to be considered. They are, briefly:

(1) If Labour is to grow, where are the additional votes to come from?

(2) Does Labour, in order to grow, need to 'target' one of the existing parties?

(3) What does Labour advise its supporters to do with their lower preferences at election time?

One answer to the first question is implicit in the anti-coalition stance: that these votes should be repossessed from Fine Gael, whither they have drifted during the period when Labour was selling its soul for office. There is a difficulty in logic about this position. It tends to assume that voters who have left Labour because of its pro-coalition stance will return once it sheds the coalition mantle—even though Fine Gael, the party to which they defected, is even more strongly in favour of coalition. But answering the coalition question before answering the other question is putting the cart before the horse.

Probably the most common assumption, however, is that if Labour again portrays itself in its truly socialist colours, it doesn't much matter where the votes come from: they will come. This approach presupposes a general attrition of support from all the other parties, perhaps roughly in proportion to the degree to which they have tended to attract traditional Labour voters—or people who ought to be traditional Labour voters. Thus, we can expect a prospectively larger erosion of votes from Fianna Fail to Labour than from Fine Gael, and the eventual extinction of the Workers' Party. The problem about this fuzzy sort of expectation is that it does not suggest any very obvious strategy. It implies, more-over, an evolving political situation in which the larger two parties (and perhaps the Workers' Party) shrink at differential rates, until there are three major parties, all roughly the same size, without any

181

single party having an overall majority in the Dail.

Labour would then have the balance of power—but so would each of the other parties, and Labour would still not be excused from having to decide, even if only intermittently, which of the others it would support, as a partner in government, as a partner outside government, or whatever. It is in this context, in particular, that the emergence of the Progressive Democrats is important. If this new political factor prevents any one party from achieving an overall majority for the next couple of elections, the choices facing Labour will be infinitely more varied than they have been in the past, and will demand new strategies. Labour's own seat potential may also be seriously affected by the emergence of the Progressive Democrats, not because the Progressive Democrats will take Labour's first preferences, but because it will attract second preferences from Fine Gael voters whose prime objective is to stop Mr Haughey's Fianna Fail rather than to elect Labour members of the Dail.

The risks involved in a decision by Labour to 'target' one of the other major parties as the focus for its electoral strategy are undoubtedly substantial. Such a strategy involves the possible loss of existing seats—and Dail seats, it will be remembered, are the hard currency of politics. Their occupants will hardly be in favour of such a strategy: the TD has not yet been born who will willingly surrender a seat in the interests of the march towards socialism, or indeed of anything else. And the influence of incumbent TDs on the party at large is much too substantial to be readily discounted. There is also the very real consideration that, regardless of the party's stated strategy on coalition, a decision to 'target' a particular party would effectively rule out coalition with that party, even though it would not necessarily rule out support for a minority government.

Even if Labour were agreed on the desirability of targetting Fianna Fail or Fine Gael, which party should it be? Fianna Fail, because it has provided an inappropriate refuge for so many people who ought to be voting Labour? Fine Gael, because it is (still) smaller than Fianna Fail, and therefore possibly more vulnerable? Are the parties really indistinguishable in ideological terms, as Labour orthodoxy would have it (in which case it does not matter from an ideological point of view which one is singled out for such a campaign)? Or is there evidence that one of them is more progressive than the other, and does therefore have to make a choice on ideological grounds? Finally, in making a choice in this situation, should Labour attack the more progressive of the two major parties in order to try and capture a liberal middle-class vote, or should it attack the more conservative one because the target, like Everest, bestrides the landscape so dramatically?

The absence of a decision to target any party in particular has the advantage of not ruling out any post-election options. Even a policy of targeting Fine Gael on the economic policy issues, and Fianna Fail on the social policy ones, would be better than generalised defence (if Labour happens to be in government) or generalised opposition (if it happens to be out of power). One of the defects of the Killarney strategy, it can be argued with the benefit of hindsight, is that it prevented Labour from embarrassing its partner in opposition (Fine Gael) except on the two high-profile issues of divorce and neutrality, because of the possibility that it might end up sharing Cabinet seats with the same party after the next election, as indeed happened.

Whether a particular party is targeted or not, the question of what Labour voters should do with their lower preferences at election times is still vital. In the last three general elections no explicit instructions on transfers were given by the party. The truth, of course, is that none were needed. In the political circumstances of the time, Labour voters, by and large, felt little difficulty in replicating the pattern to which they had become accustomed since 1973, and allocating their lower preferences to Fine Gael as the party which was (a) going to keep Mr Haughey out of power, and (b) offer to implement at least some Labour policies in government.

If the party is seriously interested in achieving the balance of power then tactical considerations suggest a fairly simple strategy. It is this: that, just as Labour's achievement of the balance of power is threatened by the likelihood of another party securing an overall majority, the prime objective of that strategy must be to prevent any party securing such a majority. Consequently, Labour votes should be cast in such a way as to deny seats to the party most likely to secure an overall majority—Fianna Fail, possibly, but, given the fortunes of politics, it could as easily be Fine Gael. Nor is there anything to be lost, and possibly a lot to be gained, if Labour voters transfer in the first instance to Workers' Party candidates or even to independent candidates with a decent record on social and economic issues. If such candidates are elected with the help of Labour transfers, some gains will have been made by the Left, however small. If they are eliminated, the lower transfers will come into play. And these transfers can be allocated, in a quite cold-blooded and public way, first to the more working-class candidates within the large party least likely to secure an overall majority, then to the other candidates of that party, and perhaps finally to the more left-wing candidates of the party most likely to return to the Dail with the largest number of seats.

This involves a degree of sophistication which is by no means foreign to the Irish electorate, and in fact offers Labour voters the possibility of making their transfers effective in a way which has never happened before. It would involve a keen assessment of the candidates being put forward by the different parties in each constituency in which Labour is putting forward its candidates, and might well call for specific recommendations for Labour voters in each constituency, creating a varying pattern of Labour transfers across the country. This strategy has nothing to do with coalition, with sentiment, with history, or with any other side issue: it is aimed solely at securing the balance of power for Labour. It could have the added advantage of focusing attention on socialist issues in the public mind in each constituency by forcing an auction between candidates of the rival larger parties who are anxious to benefit from Labour transfers. And it will mean also that, the more progressive candidates are elected to the larger parties, the more the tensions will rise in those parties between the conservative and progressive groupings.

The critical aspect of any strategy is that it is only a strategy: that transferring to Fine Gael, or to anyone else, does not necessarily imply a willingness or even a desire to support that party in government, but merely a desire to achieve greater power for the Labour Party, either in the short (balance of power) term, or in the longer view (Labour vs. Fianna Fail). But what about Fine Gael? Faced with such duplicity on the part of their former coalition partners, would their supporters refuse to turn the other cheek, and simply plump for their own candidates, or—worse again—transfer elsewhere? All of this is possible, and Labour of all parties would be wise to assume that Fine Gael voters, not to mention everyone else, will operate with their own interests in mind—not Labour's.

It is hardly surprising that, faced with such a bewildering variety of options, Labour has preferred to boil them all down to one grossly over-simplified but fatally attractive formula: is the vote in favour of coalition—or against? And it is difficult not to conclude that the debate will remain like this, ultimately arid and unsatisfying to all but the most addicted punters inside and outside the party, until questions like the above have been raised, even if they have not all been satisfactorily answered.

Among the various scenarios on offer to the Labour Party in the future, two stand out with some clarity. One is that the party should continue broadly on its present course, with an increasingly embattled leadership more and more consumed by the driving need to construct a conference majority in favour of coalition every three years—and after every election. This is a process which will, undoubtedly, devour energies which could and should be put to much better use building up the party organisation and winning Dail and local authority seats. Such a policy might even bring about further Labour Party participation in government within a reasonably short time—but would it solve any of the party's underlying problems?

The time has come, I believe, for the party to look realistically at the option of support for a minority government. The reasons are various. For one thing, the emergence of the Progressive Democrats, the growth of the Workers' Party, and Sinn Fein's nibbling at the electoral carrot, have all created a situation more akin to that which existed in the 1940s than at any time in the previous two decades. The growth of minor parties, if the experience of the 1940s is anything to go by, is actually a period of opportunity for Labour. Secondly, the brief experience of the Workers' Party, when they supported Mr Haughey's minority government of 1981–82, provides some evidence that the public is sensitive enough to the difficulties of a party in such a situation. The Workers' Party suffered at the first 1982 election, it is true, but arguably much less than had they been in coalition with Fianna Fail. There is nothing like the sight of a ministry, with all the emoluments that accompany it, to evoke every last ounce of anti-establishment feeling in the breast of the average Irish voter in hard times. And in such hard times, eaten bread is soon forgotten. The increases in social welfare payments that Labour may have

185

fought for or achieved in government are either ignored or—worse—depicted as part of a further assault by this party on hard-pressed PAYE workers in order to further subsidise the shiftless and the socially inadequate. And its failure to deliver on other policies—such as divorce—is if anything magnified by the public perception of its powerlessness.

In government or out, Labour certainly needs to tackle the problem of its poor image, not all of which can be put down to a hostile media or an indifferent electorate. In government, especially, Labour needs to look at methods of heightening the party's public profile—by having a more aggressive, public, general secretary on continental lines, for example. Equally, the traditions of Irish cabinet government can and should be structurally challenged by a minority government party. In 1975, for instance, a Labour initiative to present an alternative economic strategy to cabinet, after considerable planning, was thwarted when the cabinet as a whole decided that Brendan Corish, as Minister for Health and Social Welfare (i.e., a non-economic ministry) did not have the right to introduce a major economic policy document. If the function of Irish cabinet traditions is to confine Labour ministers to traditional, 'welfarist' ghettos, then either the traditions must be changed (and a proper *cabinet* system introduced) or Labour must decide that the price of power is too high.

The problem is essentially a tactical one: how does the party move from being in government to a position in which it will not enter government but may support one party or another as part of a minority government? On the assumption that no issue will arise between now (mid-1985) and the next general election which will provoke an actual rupture and therefore solve the problem for Labour, the steps taken by the leadership are critical. Ideally, too, whatever, steps are taken should be part of a leadership initiative —not forced on an unwilling leader and PLP by an angry and agressive conference. The political losses of such a procedure have already been amply demonstrated by the Michael O'Leary debacle.

If the needs of the party and the people it represents are paramount, it should not be impossible for the leadership at some stage to declare that the task of re-organising and strengthening the party can best be done out of government and that therefore, while continuing to fight for the interests of those it represents in the Dail, Labour should not form part of any coalition for the next two elections. Such a period would have two advantages. It would be long enough to ensure that the party was given a reasonable opportunity to prove itself out of government, and it would be short enough to maintain the involvement and commitment of those party members to whom raw anti-coalitionism is a political cul-de-sac.

Abstaining from coalition, of course, does not necessarily mean abstaining from power, and those hardy Labour TDs charged with carrying out such a policy in the Dail will find that supporting a government—any government—from the outside, as a party holding the balance of power inevitably has to, is harder on the arteries than almost any other form of political activity. They will also discover—if they were not already aware of it—that if you hold the balance of power there is, quite simply, no such thing as 'socialist opposition', unless that term can be expanded to include occasionally voting with the government of the day, or abstaining in situations in which a general election is not thereby precipitated: And where abstention is concerned, they will find that it is at best a temporary expedient, and that come Budget Day or other major occasions, the electorate will be decreasingly impressed by parliamentary abstention, however noble a gesture it may seem to the abstainer. The choice all too frequently is between two different sets of consequences, one of them only marginally less unpleasant than the other.

If the leadership has to face up to the fact that participation in coalition, no matter what achievements have been chalked up, has not worked to help the party grow to the point where it can begin to exercise real power, party activists for their part also have some dilemmas with which to come to terms. They should recognise, for instance, that annual conference is a very blunt instrument, and that it may be inappropriate to wield it in some of the delicately-timed and sensitive areas of parliamentary politics.

The bottom line, which Dick Spring as leader of the Labour Party undoubtedly accepts, and which any leader of the party would reject at their peril, is that it should be unthinkable for the PLP to enter coalition without an explicit mandate to that effect from a special conference of the party. That precedent, at least, has been firmly established now for a decade or so. But is it necessarily the case that the party should involve itself in a special delegate conference after every election in which no party has an overall majority? For one thing, it may be quite unclear in such a situation even up to the time the Dail meets, what the outcome of its deliberations and votes will be. And, if the party leadership cannot predict them, how can a party conference prescribe for them?

My argument, essentially, is that whereas coalition is too big a decision to be left to the PLP, conference should be mature enough—and accept the constitutional realities of the situation with sufficient openness—to accept that lesser parliamentary decisions, taken in fluctuating and uncertain circumstances, are normally best taken by the men and women to whom they have entrusted the task of acting as Labour public representatives. It may well be the case that the party as a whole may lose confidence in some or all of its public representatives—including its leader—even in a non-coalition situation. But the answer to this problem is a time-honoured one which has to some degree fallen out of favour in Irish politics: de-selection of the offending representative concerned, or the passage of a vote of no confidence at the annual conference itself.

In the last analysis, the quality of the Labour Party, in or out of government, supporting a minority government or in 'socialist opposition', is determined by the quality of the men and women chosen by its activists to go before the electorate in its name. For the party to take political failure out on its TDs when the remedy lies in its own hands is an exercise in political circularity. If the Labour Party as a whole wants socialists in the Dail, it will have to make sure that they get there, and in sufficient numbers. And if the party fails in this primary task, it will have no-one to blame but itself.

Index